HOW TO RAISE GOOD HUMANS WITH SUPERPOWER LIFE SKILLS

A PARENT'S GUIDE TO RAISING KIND, RESPONSIBLE, AND CONFIDENT KIDS—ONE SUPERPOWER AT A TIME

MIKE KLAASSEN

Paperback edition ISBN: 9798992952100
eBook edition ISBN: 9798992952117
Hardcover edition ISBN: 9798992952124

ACKNOWLEDGMENTS

I thank my wife, Gerri, for her loving support and encouragement, which made this book possible. I also appreciate the encouragement and support of my friend and fellow author, L. D. Alford.

Dedicated to parents, grandparents, guardians, teachers, coaches, counselors, mentors, and other adult leaders committed to raising mindful, responsible, and well-rounded children.

CONTENTS

INTRODUCTION

This may be one of the most important books you'll ever read about your role in shaping young lives. As a proud father and grandfather, I can't help but wish my wife and I had this guide when we were raising our own kids.

If you're like me, some of your earliest memories involve watching a man in a red cape soar through the sky, bend steel bars with his bare hands, and see through walls with X-ray vision. Superheroes have long captured our imagination, shaping how we define strength, courage, and victory. But this book isn't about fictional heroes—it's about the real-life superheroes your children can become. Not by leaping tall buildings or swinging between skyscrapers, but by mastering the skills that lead to a fulfilling, successful life.

Imagine your children waking up each day with a sense of purpose, confidence, and excitement—ready to take on life's challenges. This book isn't just about helping them get by—it equips them to thrive. Packed with practical strategies and empowering insights, it provides the tools children need to develop essential life skills like habit management, emotional intelligence, and leadership. Whether their aspirations lie in academic achievement, personal growth, or future career success, this book serves as a roadmap to becoming their own kind of superhero.

THE CHALLENGES OF MODERN CHILDHOOD

In today's fast-paced, hyper-connected world, childhood comes with unprecedented challenges. Young people face identity struggles, mental health concerns, and the relentless pressures of digital communication. Anxiety and depression are on the rise, and cyberbullying has become a growing threat to today's youth. Amid these issues, children must juggle academics, friendships, and family expectations—all while trying to find their place in the world.[1]

This book provides the tools to help them navigate and overcome these challenges. Throughout my life, I've seen firsthand the ups and downs of growing up in an ever-changing world. My goal is to share hard-earned insights that will empower you to guide your children toward a life of confidence, resilience, and success. Together, we'll explore essential life skills that can turn this turbulent phase into a period of growth, strength, and self-discovery.

LIFE SKILLS AS SUPERPOWERS

Strategic life skills, or "superpowers," are the cornerstones of personal and professional success. These skills extend far beyond academic achievements, encompassing the real-world competencies necessary for navigating life's complexities.[2] This book covers seven categories of superpowers:

- Holistic Well-Being
- Core Personal Development
- Analytical and Decision-Making Skills
- Communication and Interpersonal Skills
- Leadership and Teamwork
- Practical Life Management
- Technology and Learning Skills

Each superpower equips children with the tools to thrive in a challenging world and positively impact those around them.

WHY START NOW?

You might wonder if one book can adequately cover such a broad range of topics, or if your children are too young to learn about strategic life skills. Rest assured, this book isn't about instant transformation—it's about laying a solid foundation for lifelong growth. The insights provided offer immediate benefits while setting the stage for deeper exploration over time.

A UNIQUE RESOURCE

Could you find all this information elsewhere? Of course. But this book distills a wealth of knowledge into a cohesive framework, saving you time and effort while giving your children a head start. It's designed to be both a comprehensive guide and a handy reference, offering insights you can return to as new challenges arise.

PROGRESS, NOT PERFECTION

Parenting is a journey—not a sprint. You don't need to rush through this book. Take it one superpower at a time. Reflect on the lessons, practice the strategies, and let the insights settle in. If you want more information or ideas, consult the end notes and bibliography. Remember Desmond Tutu's wise words: "There's only one way to eat an elephant—a bite at a time."

Change takes time and effort. Some changes will come quickly—others will require persistence. Focus on small, manageable steps. Celebrate progress, no matter how incremental. Every positive change strengthens the foundation for your children's growth.

THE HERO'S JOURNEY

Like the heroes of our favorite stories, parents and children face trials and triumphs. Each step in mastering these life skills is a stride toward realizing potential. As Luke Skywalker of *Star Wars* discovered his power through perseverance, your children can develop their superpowers with your guidance and support.

This book is your invitation to embark on a transformative journey. Together, we'll help your children unlock their extraordinary potential and become the best version of themselves.

The first chapter begins with holistic well-being, where we will explore stress management, wellness management, self-reflection, and mindfulness.

HOLISTIC WELL-BEING

H *olistic well-being* refers to a balanced state of health that encompasses not just the physical but also the mental and emotional dimensions of life. It involves taking care of your body through proper nutrition, exercise, and sleep, while also nurturing your mind and emotions. Holistic well-being recognizes that all these areas are interconnected, and achieving harmony contributes to an overall sense of balance and fulfillment.[1]

Imagine Batman, who, after a night of outwitting villains and safeguarding the city, still dedicates time to physical training and mindfulness.[2] This iconic superhero understands the importance of holistic well-being—balancing the intense stress of crime-fighting with personal health and mental clarity. The superhuman ability to manage stress, maintain peak physical condition, and stay mentally sharp is not just for the comics—it's a model of self-care and resilience that your children can also master.

This chapter focuses on stress management, wellness management, self-reflection, and mindfulness—essential life skills for thriving in today's fast-paced world. As we explore these superpowers, remember that your journey to holistic well-being is uniquely yours. There's no one-size-fits-all approach—what works well for one person may not be the best fit for another, and that's perfectly okay. Take in the ideas presented, experiment with different strategies, and choose what resonates most with you and your family. By helping children engage with these practices, you empower them to take charge of their own well-being, building a foundation for a life of balance, health, and fulfillment.

Let's begin our journey by exploring the superpower of stress management.

SUPERPOWER #1: STRESS MANAGEMENT

Stress management is the ability to recognize, control, and reduce the impact of stress on your mind and body. It involves understanding the sources of stress, identifying how it affects you physically and emotionally, and applying various techniques to manage those effects.[3]

We live in a world where stress has become an accepted part of daily life. Occasional stress can be beneficial, pushing you to stay motivated and accomplish tasks. But chronic or prolonged stress can take a serious toll on both your mental and physical well-being. If you've been experiencing sleep difficulties, muscle tension, or frequent headaches, stress may be the culprit.[4]

Research shows that when we're under intense amounts of stress, more cortisol (the stress hormone) is released in our body, which can increase heart rate and blood pressure, possibly leading to heart disease.[5] Mentally, constant stress can increase the risk of anxiety and depression.[6]

As a parent, mastering stress management is not only vital for your own health but also for setting a positive example for your children. By demonstrating healthy ways to cope with stress, you teach them that challenges can be handled without being consumed by worry or frustration. This skill becomes a valuable tool that they can carry with them throughout their lives.

Training Missions for Children

Here are some activities children can engage in to learn how to manage stress effectively.

- **Mindful breathing exercises.** Teach children simple breathing exercises to help them calm down when they feel stressed. Encourage them to take deep, slow breaths, counting to four as they inhale and exhale. Practicing this regularly can help them manage anxiety and stay centered during challenging situations.[7]
- **Journaling for stress relief.** Encourage children to keep a journal where they can write or draw about their feelings. Provide prompts like "What made you feel stressed today?" or "How did you handle a tough situation?" Journaling allows children to process their emotions, identify stressors, and reflect on how they can manage their feelings more effectively.[8]
- **Physical activity breaks.** Promote regular physical activity as a way to reduce stress. Encourage children to engage in activities they enjoy, like playing sports, dancing, or riding a bike. Physical exercise releases endorphins, which help improve mood and reduce stress levels.[9]
- **Creative expression.** Provide opportunities for children to express their feelings through art, music, or writing. Whether it's drawing a picture, playing an instrument, or writing a story, creative outlets allow children to release stress and explore their emotions in a positive way.[10]

- **Positive visualization.** Teach children the technique of positive visualization, where they imagine themselves in a peaceful and happy place, such as a favorite park or a quiet beach. Guide them through visualizing the sights, sounds, and feelings of being in that place. Visualization helps shift focus away from stress and brings a sense of calm and relaxation.[11]
- **Time management skills.** Guide children to master time management to help them stay organized and avoid feeling overwhelmed. Encourage them to break tasks into smaller, manageable steps and to prioritize their responsibilities. Use checklists or planners to help them stay organized, which can reduce stress caused by procrastination or feeling unprepared.[12]
- **Talking about feelings.** Create a safe space for children to talk about their feelings and stressors. Encourage open communication and let them know it's okay to feel stressed sometimes. Offer reassurance and help them brainstorm solutions to their challenges. Knowing they have support can significantly reduce their stress levels.[13]

These practices equip children with lifelong skills to navigate the ups and downs of life with confidence and calm.

In the 2012 film *The Dark Knight Rises*, Bruce Wayne (Batman) faces immense pressure as Gotham descends into chaos under Bane's control. Despite being physically broken and imprisoned, Bruce remains composed, methodically planning his return. His exceptional stress management is evident when he escapes the prison, regains his physical strength, and devises a strategy to defeat Bane. This illustrates how Batman stays calm and focused, using resilience and mental discipline to manage extreme stress and push forward in the face of over-whelming adversity.[14]

Mastering the superpower of stress management is essential for your children's overall well-being and future success. Teaching children to recognize and manage stress equips them with the resilience they need to face life's inevitable challenges with confidence. Your children will learn to maintain balance and composure in the face of adversity through practical activities and strategies that promote mindfulness, emotional regulation, and a healthy lifestyle. This superpower not only strengthens their emotional intelligence but also lays the foundation for a lifetime of well-being and effective problem-solving.

ACTION ITEMS

- Before you read further, take a few minutes to consider the information presented in this section.
- Take a moment to identify the types and causes of stress in your children's life.
- Imagine your children decades in the future (after many years of cultivating stress-management skills) and how they use this superpower to achieve their goals.
- Note how your children currently employ stress management in their daily life. Take pride in the progress they've already achieved in developing this superpower.
- Evaluate the effectiveness of your current practices to help your children cultivate these skills.
- If you decide that your current efforts to help your children cultivate stress management need to be improved, consider at least one improvement you can make in the coming weeks, months, or year.
- Develop a plan for implementing that improvement.

Now that we've addressed stress management, let's move on to the superpower life skill of wellness management.

SUPERPOWER #2: WELLNESS MANAGEMENT

Wellness management is the ability to maintain a balanced and healthy lifestyle by focusing on diet, exercise, and sleep. Together, these three elements form the foundation of a well-rounded approach to physical and mental well-being.[15]

Mastering wellness management is crucial for parents, not just for their own health but also for setting a positive example for their children. By demonstrating the importance of caring for one's body through good nutrition, physical activity, and rest, you show your kids that wellness is a key component of living a happy and successful life.

In this chapter, we'll explore strategies and activities to help your family develop the superpower of wellness management. From preparing healthy meals to staying active as a family and establishing good sleep routines, these practices will empower everyone to lead a healthier, more vibrant life.

Eating Nutritious Food

Consuming the right nutrients is essential for unlocking your superpowers. Think of your body as a high-performance machine needing premium fuel. Eating nutritious food can significantly improve your life in multiple ways. A diet rich in essential nutrients like omega-3 fatty acids,[16] antioxidants,[17] and vitamins helps boost brain function by enhancing memory, concentration, and cognitive abilities. With fruits, vegetables, lean proteins, and whole grains, you'll fuel your brain to perform at its best, helping you think strategically and stay sharp.[18]

Eating well also boosts your energy levels. By providing your body with a balanced mix of carbohydrates, proteins, and fats, you can maintain a steady supply of energy throughout the day, avoiding the crashes that come from sugary snacks and processed foods.[19] Additionally, a nutritious diet positively affects your mood and mental health. Certain foods can increase serotonin levels, which help promote happiness and well-being while reducing the effects of stress, anxiety, and depression.[20]

Good nutrition strengthens your immune system as well, making you less vulnerable to illnesses. Antioxidant-rich foods, along with essential vitamins and minerals, provide your body with the defenses it needs to fight off infections.[21] On a physical level, a balanced diet improves your fitness and endurance by providing the necessary nutrients like protein for muscle repair and growth,[22] and calcium and iron to keep your bones strong.[23]

In the long run, consistently eating nutritious foods can reduce your risk of chronic diseases like obesity, type 2 diabetes, heart disease, and certain cancers. By making healthy eating a priority, you create the foundation for a more vibrant and healthier life.[24]

The Skinny on Fats

When it comes to dietary fats, the Mayo Clinic[25] explains that there are two primary categories: saturated fats and unsaturated fats, which are further divided into monounsaturated fats and polyunsaturated fats. Each type affects our bodies differently, and most foods contain a blend of these fats. While some fats are essential for healthy cell function, others can increase the risk of disease. So, how do we know which fats to include in our diet and which to limit?

The Mayo Clinic offers these straightforward tips for making healthier choices about fats.

- **Opt for plant-based oils.** Instead of using butter or lard, try sautéing vegetables with olive oil. For high-heat cooking like stir-frying or searing, canola oil is a good choice.
- **Incorporate fish into your diet.** Especially good is oily fish like salmon, which is rich in heart-healthy omega-3 fatty acids.
- **Choose lean meats and skinless poultry.** Trim visible fat from cuts of meat and remove skin from poultry to reduce saturated fat intake.
- **Go for low-fat dairy products.** Swap full-fat options for lower-fat alternatives in milk, yogurt, and cheese.
- **Snack smart with whole fruits and vegetables.** They're filling, nutritious, and naturally low in unhealthy fats.
- **Limit processed foods.** Many are packed with unhealthy saturated fats, so choose fresh options whenever possible.
- **Read labels carefully.** Even low-fat or fat-free processed foods can be loaded with added sugars and sodium, so checking the nutrition information is important.

By making these small adjustments, you can enjoy the benefits of healthy fats while controlling less desirable ones. [26]

Tips for a Balanced Diet

- **Drink water.** Stay hydrated by drinking water throughout the day. Add some fruit slices to make things interesting.[27]
- **Eat three meals a day.** Ensure your body gets the energy and nutrients it needs.[28]

- **Include healthy snacks.** Choose fruits, vegetables, nuts, or yogurt instead of starchy or sugary foods.[29]
- **Increase your fiber intake.** Consume whole grains, fruits, vegetables, and legumes.[30]
- **Decrease your salt intake.** Cut back on salty foods and choose low-sodium options.[31]
- **Eat balanced meals.** Mix protein, carbohydrates, and healthy fats in each meal.[32]
- **Choose healthier cooking methods.** Try baking, broiling, or grilling instead of frying.[33]
- **Be mindful of added sugars.** Reduce sugar intake and watch for hidden sugars in snacks and drinks.[34]
- **Eat lean meats.** Opt for lean cuts of meat, including chicken and fish.[35]
- **Prepare your meals.** Learn to prepare simple, healthy meals.[36]

Fueling your body with the right nutrients is essential for unlocking your superpowers. A diet rich in essential nutrients lays the foundation for a healthier, more vibrant life.

Training Missions for Children

Here are some activities children can engage in to cultivate the superpower of wellness management through eating nutritious food.

- **Healthy cooking classes.** Involve children in the kitchen by teaching them how to prepare simple, healthy meals and snacks. Let them pick out fruits, vegetables, and other nutritious ingredients, and guide them through the process of making a meal. Cooking together not only teaches valuable life skills but also encourages a positive relationship with healthy foods.[37]

- **Nutrition rainbow challenge.** Encourage children to eat a variety of colorful fruits and vegetables by turning it into a game. Challenge them to eat a "rainbow" of different colors each day—red tomatoes, orange carrots, yellow bananas, green spinach, and so on. Keeping track of their progress with a colorful chart can make it fun and rewarding to try new foods.[38]

- **Garden-to-table experience.** If possible, start a small garden where children can grow their own fruits, vegetables, or herbs. Involve them in every step, from planting seeds to harvesting the produce. Eating food they've grown themselves can be a powerful motivator for children to enjoy and appreciate nutritious foods.[39]

- **Supermarket scavenger hunt.** Turn grocery shopping into an educational experience with a supermarket scavenger hunt. Give children a list of healthy foods to find, such as whole grains, leafy greens, or protein-rich foods. Explain the benefits of each food item as they check it off their list, teaching them how to make healthy choices when shopping.[40]

- **Learning about food labels.** Teach children how to read and understand food labels. Show them how to identify important information such as serving size, ingredients, and nutrient content. This knowledge empowers them to make informed choices about what they eat, helping them to recognize nutritious options.[41]

- **Healthy snack prep.** Encourage children to prepare their own healthy snacks, like fruit and yogurt parfaits, veggie sticks with hummus, or homemade trail mix. This approach not only makes healthy eating more enjoyable but also empowers them to make nutritious choices independently.[42]

- **Mindful eating practices.** Introduce the concept of mindful eating, where children focus on the taste, texture, and smell of their food while eating slowly and without distractions. Encourage them to listen to their bodies, recognizing when they're hungry or full. This practice helps build a healthy relationship with food and prevents overeating.[43]

By participating in these activities, children can develop physical health and also lay the foundation for lifelong healthy eating habits.

Exercising Regularly

Batman doesn't just rely on his gadgets—his physical fitness is a core part of his ability to fight crime. By incorporating exercise into his daily routine, he maintains peak physical condition, much like how you can use regular physical activity to stay energized and focused.

Regular exercise can significantly enhance your life in numerous ways. It boosts brain health by improving cognitive functions such as attention, memory, and problem-solving skills. You'll find that staying active sharpens your focus and mental clarity, helping you perform better in both academic and everyday tasks.[44]

Exercise also plays a key role in managing your weight. By burning calories, increasing your metabolism, and building muscle mass, it helps you maintain a healthy body composition.[45] Beyond weight management, regular exercise reduces your risk of various diseases. It lowers blood pressure, improves cholesterol levels, and decreases the likelihood of developing cardiovascular conditions, type 2 diabetes, and metabolic syndrome.[46]

Strengthening your bones and muscles is another vital benefit of regular exercise. Weight-bearing activities like running and strength training help fortify your bones and build muscle, making you physically stronger and more resilient. In addition, regular exercise enhances your overall fitness, making everyday activities easier to perform and allowing you to tackle physical challenges with greater ease.[47]

By embracing exercise, you improve your physical health, sharpen your mind, and elevate your daily performance.

Tips for Regular Physical Activity

- **Learn simple exercises.** Do bodyweight exercises like lunges, squats, pushups, and hip hinges.[48]
- **Engage in different types of exercise.** Include resistance training, cardio, and high-intensity interval training (HIIT).[49]
- **Commit to sixty minutes of exercise daily.** These activities may include jogging, swimming, dancing, sports, or brisk walking.[50]
- **Find enjoyable activities.** Make physical activity a sustainable and enjoyable part of your routine.[51]

Increasing Your Physical Activity

There's no need to go overboard and start an exercise regimen that is impossible for you to maintain. You can start, for example, with a brisk 10-minute walk each day and gradually increase the amount of time.[52] Things like taking the stairs instead of the elevator and carrying grocery bags can all help.

Technology is awesome for physical activity. Apps like FitOn are free to join and offer many different types of exercises for different levels and lengths of time. This makes exercising more convenient and easier to incorporate into your daily routine.

To ensure you're taking part in a variety of physical activities, use the following ideas to create a personalized workout that you love.

Aerobic	Muscle Strengthening	Bone Strengthening
Swimming	Sit-ups	Walking
Running	Push-ups	Hiking
Cycling	Squats	Skipping rope
Skating	Pilates	Yoga
Jumping jacks	Rock climbing	Gymnastics
Team sports	Skiing	Volleyball
Dancing	Surfing	Lunges
Boxing	Weightlifting	Tennis

Finally, always make sure you warm up and cool down properly and keep hydrated while you're exercising.

Training Missions for Children

Here are some activities children can engage in to cultivate the superpower of wellness management through regular exercise.

- **Active playtime.** Encourage children to spend time each day engaging in active play. Physical activity is a fun and regular part of their routine, whether it's playing tag, riding bikes, jumping rope, or playing sports. Active play not only promotes fitness but also helps develop coordination, strength, and social skills.[53]
- **Outdoor adventures.** Plan regular outdoor activities like hiking, swimming, or playing at the park. Exploring nature not only provides physical exercise but also allows

children to connect with the environment and enjoy the benefits of being outdoors. Encourage them to try new activities like climbing or kayaking to keep things exciting.[54]

- **Sports and extracurricular Activities.** Encourage children to participate in sports or other physical extracurricular activities, such as gymnastics, martial arts, or dance. These activities provide structured opportunities for regular exercise and help children develop discipline, teamwork, and a love for physical fitness.[55]
- **Yoga and stretching.** Introduce children to yoga and stretching exercises that they can do daily. Yoga helps improve flexibility, strength, and mindfulness, making it a great way to incorporate both physical and mental wellness into their routine. Consider practicing yoga together as a calming way to start or end the day.[56]
- **Movement breaks during study time.** Incorporate short movement breaks during homework or study sessions. Encourage children to stand up, stretch, or do a quick set of exercises like squats or push-ups. These breaks help keep their bodies active and their minds focused, reducing the stress of long periods of sitting.[57]
- **Tracking progress with a fitness journal.** Provide children with a fitness journal where they can track their physical activities, set exercise goals, and reflect on how they feel after exercising. Reviewing their progress regularly can motivate them to stay consistent and celebrate their achievements in building a healthy, active lifestyle.[58]

These practices not only enhance their physical health but also build the foundation for a lifelong habit of staying active and enjoying the benefits of movement.

Getting Enough Sleep

Getting enough sleep can enhance your life in multiple ways. Sleep is essential for maintaining physical health, as it allows your body to repair tissues, build muscle, and strengthen the immune system, ensuring that you wake up ready to take on the day. Adequate sleep also sharpens your mental clarity, improving your ability to concentrate, make decisions, and solve problems more effectively.[59]

Emotionally, sleep plays an important role in managing stress and helping you maintain a positive outlook. You're better equipped to handle challenges and stay emotionally balanced when well-rested.[60] Additionally, sleep boosts creativity, providing your brain with the necessary time to recharge and enabling you to excel in creative pursuits.[61] Establishing a healthy sleep routine not only helps you perform better day-to-day but also sets the foundation for long-term success, allowing you to pursue your ambitions with the energy, clarity, and resilience needed to achieve your goals.

Tips to Improve Sleep

- **Budget enough time for sleep.** Aim for eight to ten hours, even on weekends.
- **Establish a pre-bed routine.** Engage in relaxing activities like reading or mindfulness practice.
- **Limit caffeine and energy drinks.** Avoid these stimulants, especially in the afternoon and evening.
- **Minimize electronic device use.** Such activities prior to bedtime may cause mental stimulation that is hard to reverse.[62]
- **Create a sleep-friendly environment.** Keep your bedroom cool, dark, and quiet.

- **Optimize your sleep surface.** Ensure your mattress and pillow are comfortable.
- **Give yourself time to wind down.** Aim for around thirty minutes to chill out before going to bed.

By following these tips, you can improve the quality of your sleep and overall well-being—and you'll get more out of the time you're awake.

Training Missions for Children

Here are some activities children can engage in to cultivate the superpower of wellness management through healthy sleep habits.

- **Establish a bedtime routine.** Work with children to create a consistent bedtime routine that they can follow every night. This might include activities like taking a warm bath, brushing their teeth, reading a book, or doing some light stretching. A calming routine signals to the body that it's time to wind down, making it easier to fall asleep and wake up feeling refreshed.[63]
- **Create a sleep-friendly environment.** Encourage children to help set up their bedroom in a way that promotes good sleep. This can include dimming the lights, keeping the room cool, and minimizing noise. They can also choose calming colors for their bedding or decorate their space with items that make them feel relaxed and secure.[64]
- **Limit screen time before bed.** Teach children about the impact of screen time on sleep and encourage them to turn off electronic devices at least an hour before bedtime. Instead of screen time, suggest engaging in quiet activities like reading, drawing, or listening to calming music. This

helps their mind and body prepare for a restful night's sleep.[65]

- **Sleep diary.** Introduce the idea of a sleep diary where children can track their sleep patterns. Have them note when they go to bed, when they wake up, and how they feel in the morning. Reviewing the sleep diary together can help identify any patterns or habits affecting their sleep and encourage them to adjust for better rest.[66]

- **Teach relaxation techniques.** Show children simple relaxation techniques they can use if they're having trouble falling asleep, such as deep breathing exercises, progressive muscle relaxation, or visualization of a peaceful place. These techniques help calm the mind and body, making it easier to drift off to sleep.[67]

- **Talk about the benefits of sleep.** Discuss the benefits of getting enough sleep, such as feeling more energized, being able to concentrate better at school, and having a stronger immune system. Helping children understand why sleep is important can motivate them to prioritize their bedtime routine.[68]

- **Sleep-friendly nutrition.** Encourage children to avoid heavy meals, sugary snacks, or caffeine close to bedtime. Teach them about foods that can promote better sleep, such as a small snack of whole grains, dairy, or fruits like bananas. Making healthy food choices in the evening supports a good night's rest.[69]

By engaging in these practices, children not only enhance their physical health and mental clarity but also set the foundation for a lifetime of healthy sleep routines, which are essential for overall well-being and success.

In the 2005 film *Batman Begins*, Bruce Wayne demonstrates a deep commitment to physical and mental wellness after years of intense training. His time with the League of Shadows is marked by disciplined physical conditioning, martial arts mastery, and preparing his body for the challenges ahead. Even after assuming the mantle of Batman, Bruce follows a strict regimen, maintaining peak fitness through rigorous training, proper diet, and rest. This highlights his dedication to wellness management, ensuring his physical health is always at its best to sustain his strength and stamina.[70]

Cultivating the superpower of wellness management is vital for your children's long-term health and happiness. By instilling habits of eating nutritious foods, engaging in regular exercise, and prioritizing enough sleep, you're providing them with the tools to maintain a balanced and healthy lifestyle. These practices not only support their physical well-being but also enhance their mental and emotional resilience. As they learn to care for their bodies and minds, they'll be better equipped to face life's challenges with energy, focus, and a positive outlook. This superpower is foundational for leading a fulfilling and vibrant life.

ACTION ITEMS

- Before you read further, take a few minutes to consider the information presented in this section.
- Imagine your children decades in the future (after many years of cultivating wellness-management) and how they use this superpower to achieve their goals.
- Note how your children currently employ wellness management in their daily life. Take pride in the progress they've already achieved in developing this superpower.

- Evaluate the effectiveness of your current practices to help your children cultivate these skills.
- If you decide that your current efforts to help your children cultivate wellness management need to be improved, consider at least one improvement you can make in the coming weeks, months, or year.
- Develop a plan for implementing that improvement.

Now that we have addressed wellness management, it's time to move on to the superpowers of self-reflection and mindfulness.

SUPERPOWERS #3 & 4: SELF-REFLECTION AND MINDFULNESS

In this chapter, we'll explore techniques and activities that can help your family develop the superpowers of self-reflection and mindfulness. From deep breathing to reflective journaling, these practices will empower your children to live more consciously, learn from their experiences, and find balance in a busy world.

Self-reflection and mindfulness form a powerful duo of strategic life skills. Self-reflection deepens your understanding of who you are,[71] while mindfulness centers you in the present moment, freeing you from worries about the past or future.[72] Since both of these superpowers involve your inner world, they're often mistaken for one another. To make it easier to distinguish between them, I'll explore them together in this chapter. Let's dive into what makes each unique and how they complement one another.

Self-Reflection

Self-reflection is the ability to critically examine your thoughts, actions, and experiences to better understand yourself. It involves taking time to look inward, considering your motivations, strengths, weaknesses, and the impact of your behavior on others. This superpower encourages you to pause and evaluate your past choices, habits, and emotional responses, while also considering how they shape your future decisions and actions. In self-reflection, you develop a more accurate sense of who you are, your values, and what drives your decisions. It requires honesty, introspection, and a willingness to explore your inner world to foster personal growth.[73]

Training Missions for Children to Cultivate Self-Reflection

Here are some activities children can engage in to cultivate this superpower.

- **Daily reflection journals.** Encourage children to keep a daily journal where they can reflect on their day. Ask them to write or draw about what they enjoyed, what challenged them, and what they learned. Provide prompts like, "What was the best part of your day?" or "How did you feel when something didn't go as planned?" Regular journaling helps children process their experiences and understand their emotions.[74]
- **Reflection time after activities.** After completing a significant activity, such as a school project, a sports game, or a social event, set aside time to discuss how it went. Ask questions like, "What went well?" "What could you improve next time?" and "How did you feel during the activity?" This practice encourages children to think critically about their actions and learn from their experiences.[75]
- **Reflective moments.** Introduce children to reflective practices that involve sitting quietly and reflecting on their

thoughts and feelings. Encourage them to close their eyes, take deep breaths, and think about a recent experience. Reflective moments help children develop the habit of pausing to reflect and become more aware of their inner thoughts.[76]

- **Self-reflection art projects.** Have children create art projects that express their thoughts and feelings. For example, they can draw or paint a picture that represents a recent experience or create a collage of images that reflect their current emotions. Discuss their artwork with them, asking questions that help them articulate their feelings and insights. Art provides a creative outlet for self-reflection.[77]

- **Gratitude practice.** Encourage children to practice gratitude by reflecting on things they are thankful for each day. This can be done through a gratitude journal, a family gratitude jar, or simply sharing their thoughts at the dinner table. Focusing on gratitude helps children reflect on the positive aspects of their lives and fosters a sense of appreciation.[78]

- **Goal-setting and reflection.** Help children set personal goals and regularly reflect on their progress. After achieving or working toward a goal, discuss what they learned, how they felt during the process, and what they might do differently next time. This activity teaches them to reflect on their growth and see challenges as opportunities for learning.[79]

- **Storytelling and reflection.** Share stories with children, either from books or personal experiences, and discuss the characters' actions and emotions. Ask them to reflect on what they would have done in the same situation and why. Storytelling helps children connect with different perspectives and encourages them to reflect on their own choices and values.[80]

These practices strengthen children's emotional intelligence, equipping them to learn and grow from their experiences while laying the foundation for lifelong personal development.

> In the 2008 film *The Dark Knight*, after the tragic death of Rachel Dawes, Bruce Wayne's childhood friend and love interest, he struggles with the consequences of his choices, especially the impact of his role as Batman on Gotham. Bruce embarks on a deep process of self-reflection, questioning the morality of his actions and the toll his dual life is taking. This inner conflict unfolds in conversations with Alfred, where Bruce voices his doubts and reassesses his motives. These moments of introspection highlight Bruce's capacity for self-reflection as he steps back to evaluate his purpose and the true impact of his actions.[81]

Now that we've explored self-reflection, let's turn to mindfulness.

Mindfulness

Mindfulness is the ability to be fully present and engaged in the current moment, aware of your thoughts, feelings, bodily sensations, and surroundings without judgment or distraction. It involves paying deliberate attention to your experiences as they unfold, allowing you to observe them with clarity and acceptance. This superpower encourages a heightened state of consciousness, where you can focus on the here and now rather than dwelling on the past or worrying about the future. Mindfulness often incorporates practices like deep breathing, mindful observation, and meditation to cultivate calm awareness and intentional living.[82]

Training Missions for Children to Cultivate Mindfulness

Here are some activities children can engage in to cultivate this superpower.

- **Mindful breathing exercises.** Teach children simple breathing exercises that they can use to calm their minds and focus their attention. Encourage them to take deep breaths, paying close attention to the sensation of the air entering and leaving their bodies. Practice this regularly, especially when they feel overwhelmed or anxious. Mindful breathing, such as counting to four on the inhale, helps children stay grounded and present in the moment.[83]
- **Sensory awareness walks.** Take children on a walk in nature, encouraging them to fully engage their senses. Ask them to notice the sounds of birds, the smell of flowers, the texture of leaves, and the feeling of the ground beneath their feet. This activity helps children become more aware of their surroundings and cultivates a deeper connection to the present moment.[84]
- **Mindful eating.** During meals, encourage children to eat slowly and mindfully, paying attention to each bite's taste, texture, and aroma. Ask them to notice how their food makes them feel and to express gratitude for the nourishment it provides. Mindful eating promotes a healthy relationship with food and enhances their ability to savor everyday experiences.[85]
- **Body scan technique.** Guide children through a simple body scan technique where they focus on each part of their body, starting from their toes and moving up to their head. Encourage them to notice any sensations, tension, or relaxation in each area. This practice helps children tune

into their body and recognize how their emotions might manifest physically.[86]

- **Mindful movement.** Engage children in mindful movement activities such as yoga, tai chi, or simple stretching exercises. Encourage them to pay attention to how their body moves and feels during each stretch or pose. Mindful movement helps children develop body awareness and enhances their ability to stay focused and present.[87]

These practices not only improve children's emotional well-being, but also equip them with the tools to navigate challenges with greater resilience and clarity.

In the 2016 film *Batman v Superman: Dawn of Justice*, Batman demonstrates a remarkable level of mindfulness during his training and combat scenes, particularly through his sharp focus and heightened awareness of his surroundings. His battle with Superman, for instance, demands intense concentration as he carefully anticipates each move and meticulously plans his actions amidst the chaos of the fight. Batman's mindfulness is evident in his ability to stay fully present, maintain calm under immense pressure, and engage deeply in every situation, whether strategizing or in the thick of combat.[88]

Developing the superpowers of self-reflection and mindfulness helps your children enhance their emotional and mental well-being. By teaching them to pause, reflect, and be present, you're guiding them toward a deeper understanding of themselves and the world around them. This superpower supports thoughtful decision-making, emotional regulation, and a greater awareness of their experiences. Your children will learn to navigate challenges with a calm, focused mind as they practice self-reflection and mindfulness, contributing to a balanced and fulfilling life. These skills lay a strong foundation for their personal growth and emotional resilience.

ACTION ITEMS

- Before you read further, take a few minutes to consider the information presented in this section.
- Imagine your children decades in the future (after many years of cultivating self-reflection and mindfulness) and how they use these superpowers to achieve their goals.
- Note how your children currently employ self-reflection and mindfulness in their daily life. Take pride in the progress they've already achieved in developing this superpower.
- Evaluate the effectiveness of your current practices to help your children cultivate these skills.
- If you decide that your current efforts to help your children cultivate self-reflection and mindfulness need to be improved, consider at least one improvement you can make in the coming weeks, months, or year.
- Develop a plan for implementing that improvement.

In wrapping up this chapter on holistic well-being, let's revisit our caped crusader, Batman. As the guardian of Gotham, he embodies the essence of balance, showcasing not only his prowess in battling adversaries but also his commitment to self-care and mental fortitude. Through his rigorous training regimen, meditative practices, and strategic reflections, Batman exemplifies how integrating stress management, wellness, self-reflection, and mindfulness into our daily lives empowers us to tackle challenges with resilience and grace. Just as Batman emerges from the shadows night after night, stronger and more determined, we can harness these holistic well-being superpowers to navigate life's complexities with ambition and purpose. Let the Dark Knight's dedication inspire us to cultivate a balanced, fulfilling life where our own well-being is the foundation of our personal success story.

Holistic well-being shapes how your children care for their mind and body, handle challenges, and understand themselves. When they manage stress, they respond to pressure with balance and resilience. When they practice wellness, they build habits that support their physical and mental health. When they engage in self-reflection, they gain insight into their choices, actions, and growth. And when they cultivate mindfulness, they learn to be present and appreciate each moment. By fostering these skills, you help your children develop a strong foundation for a healthy, thoughtful, and fulfilling life.

In the next chapter, we'll explore how embracing personal responsibility, strategic thinking, resilience, and creativity can further empower your children to become real-life superheroes.

2

CORE PERSONAL DEVELOPMENT

ersonal development means building your skills, knowledge, and mindset to create a strong foundation for your future. This isn't just about reaching immediate goals—it's about preparing for long-term growth and fulfillment. Think of Spider-Man, a young superhero balancing school life and extraordinary abilities. His story highlights how taking responsibility, viewing life strategically, overcoming setbacks, and thinking creatively are essential traits for heroes and anyone looking to grow and thrive.[1]

In the following pages, we'll explore the superpowers of personal responsibility, strategic thinking, resilience, and creativity. Join me now for a closer look at personal responsibility.

SUPERPOWER #5: PERSONAL RESPONSIBILITY

Personal responsibility is the ability to take ownership of your actions, your decisions, and their consequences. It involves being accountable for your choices and behaviors, understanding that your actions have an impact on yourself and others. This superpower requires self-discipline, honesty, and a willingness to admit mistakes and learn from them. Personal responsibility also includes fulfilling commitments, meeting obligations, and making decisions that align with your values. It's about recognizing that you have control over your life and making intentional choices that reflect that understanding.[2]

As you guide the young people in your life, instilling the value of personal responsibility becomes a crucial part of their development. Encourage them to reflect on their actions, understand the impact they have on themselves and others, and take ownership of their choices. This superpower will not only help them thrive in their personal endeavors but also build a foundation for becoming compassionate, thoughtful, and responsible humans.

Training Missions for Children

Here are some activities children can engage in to cultivate personal responsibility.

- **Chore charts.** Create a chore chart that assigns specific tasks to each child. Make sure the tasks are age-appropriate and include both daily and weekly responsibilities. Encourage children to complete their chores without reminders and reward them for consistent effort. This activity teaches the value of contributing to the household and being responsible for their own duties.[3]
- **Personal goal-setting.** Help children set personal goals, such as improving their grades, mastering a new skill, or saving money for something they want. Encourage them to break their goals into actionable steps and track their progress. This practice fosters a sense of ownership over

their achievements and reinforces the connection between effort and results.[4]

- **Decision-making opportunities.** Give children the opportunity to make decisions that affect their lives, such as choosing their outfits, planning their activities, or organizing their study time. Afterward, discuss the outcomes of their decisions and what they learned from the experience. This activity helps children understand the impact of their choices and the importance of being responsible for them.[5]

- **Reflection on consequences.** When children make mistakes, guide them through reflecting on the consequences of their actions. Discuss what happened, why it happened, and how they can make better choices in the future. Encourage them to take responsibility for their actions rather than blaming others. This reflection process teaches accountability and the importance of learning from mistakes.[6]

- **Taking care of belongings.** Assign children the responsibility of taking care of their own belongings, such as keeping their room tidy, organizing their school supplies, or managing their own laundry. Praise them for keeping their spaces in order and remind them of the benefits of staying organized. This practice helps children develop a sense of responsibility for their possessions and personal space.[7]

- **Community service projects.** Involve children in community service projects where they can see the impact of their actions on others. Whether it's helping out at a local charity, participating in a neighborhood cleanup, or volunteering at a food bank, these experiences teach children the importance of being responsible citizens and contributing to the well-being of their community.[8]

- **Family responsibility talks.** Hold regular family meetings where each member discusses their responsibilities, both at home and in their personal lives. Encourage open dialogue about the challenges and successes of managing these responsibilities. Support each other in finding solutions. This activity fosters a sense of accountability within the family and reinforces the idea that everyone has a role to play.[9]

By engaging in these activities, children can build character and prepare themselves to navigate life's challenges with confidence and integrity.

> In the 2002 film *Spider-Man*, after gaining his powers, Peter Parker initially uses them for personal gain, seeking fame and fortune. However, the tragic death of his Uncle Ben becomes a turning point in his life. Uncle Ben's iconic advice, "With great power comes great responsibility," resonates deeply with Peter when he realizes that his inaction allowed the criminal who killed his uncle to escape. Overcome with guilt, Peter fully accepts responsibility for his choices and commits himself to using his powers to protect others as Spider-Man. This pivotal moment highlights Peter's profound sense of personal responsibility, as he understands that his abilities are not meant for self-serving purposes, but for the greater good.[10]

Encouraging the development of personal responsibility in your children helps them understand the importance of owning their actions and decisions. By teaching them to take accountability for their choices, you are guiding them toward becoming individuals who can navigate life with integrity and reliability. Personal responsibility empowers them to manage their commitments, learn from their mistakes, and contribute positively to their community. As they embrace this superpower, your children will grow into adults who confidently meet challenges and fulfill their obligations with a strong sense of purpose and accountability.

ACTION ITEMS

- Before you read further, take a few minutes to consider the information presented in this section.
- Imagine your children decades in the future (after many years of cultivating personal responsibility) and how they use this superpower to achieve their goals.
- Note how your children currently employ personal responsibility in their daily life. Take pride in the progress they've already achieved in developing this superpower.
- Evaluate the effectiveness of your current practices to help your children cultivate these skills.
- If you decide that your current efforts to help your children cultivate personal responsibility need to be improved, consider at least one improvement you can make in the coming weeks, months, or year.
- Develop a plan for implementing that improvement.

Now that we've addressed the strategic life skill of personal responsibility, let's move on to strategic thinking.

SUPERPOWER #6: STRATEGIC THINKING

Imagine you're standing at the edge of a vast, unexplored landscape. This is your life, full of endless possibilities. To navigate this terrain, you need more than just a map—you need a clear vision of where you want to go, the ambition to pursue your goals relentlessly, and the planning to make it all happen.

- *Vision* is the ability to see beyond the present and imagine a future filled with possibilities. It's about setting your sights on what you truly want to achieve and creating a guiding star that keeps you focused, motivated, and inspired. Your vision provides direction and purpose, helping you navigate through life's uncertainties with confidence.
- *Ambition* is the fuel that powers your journey. It's that inner drive that pushes you to strive for greatness, reach higher, and push past obstacles. Ambition is about being determined to turn big dreams into reality and relentlessly pursuing your goals, no matter how challenging they may seem.
- *Planning* is the bridge that connects your vision and ambition. It's the ability to make informed decisions, set priorities, manage resources, and anticipate potential challenges. Planning involves more than organizing tasks —it's about making smart choices that pave the way for success and staying proactive to handle obstacles before they become roadblocks.

Spider-Man is a great example of a strategic thinker because, despite his raw talent and powers, he relies on his mind to solve problems and anticipate outcomes. Like Spider-Man, you can't depend on strength alone when facing tough challenges—you need strategy. His vision is to protect his city and loved ones, even if it puts him at risk. He sets clear priorities—stopping threats, saving civilians, and keeping his identity hidden. His ambition drives him to keep pushing forward, no matter how overwhelming the odds.

As you help the young people in your life develop strategic thinking, you're equipping them with the tools to approach life with foresight and intention. Teach them to define their vision, create a roadmap to achieve it, and remain flexible in their approach. By fostering this superpower, you're guiding them to become proactive, thoughtful, and successful individuals who are prepared to turn their dreams into reality.

Training Missions for Children

Here are some activities children can engage in to cultivate strategic thinking.

- **Vision board creation.** Encourage children to create a vision board that represents their dreams and aspirations. Provide materials like magazines, markers, and glue so they can cut out or draw images and words that reflect what they want to achieve. Display the vision board in their room as a daily reminder of their goals. This activity helps children visualize their future and think strategically about what they want to accomplish.[11]
- **Goal-setting workshops.** Guide children in setting specific, measurable, achievable, relevant, and time-bound (SMART) goals. Break down each goal into smaller steps and create a timeline for completing each step. Regularly review their progress and adjust the plan as needed. This practice teaches children the importance of planning and perseverance in reaching their objectives.[12]
- **Planning a project.** Involve children in planning a project, such as organizing a birthday party, building a model, or creating a garden. Encourage them to think through all the necessary steps, gather materials, and assign tasks if working with others. After completing the project, discuss what went well and what could have been improved. This hands-on experience reinforces the value of careful planning and strategic thinking.[13]

- **Problem-solving scenarios.** Present children with hypothetical scenarios that require strategic thinking to solve. For example, ask them how they would plan a road trip with a limited budget, manage a school project with a tight deadline, or solve a conflict between friends. Encourage them to outline a plan, anticipate challenges, and think creatively about solutions. These scenarios help children practice thinking ahead and making strategic decisions.[14]

- **Reflective journaling.** Encourage children to keep a journal where they reflect on their goals, plans, and the steps they are taking to achieve them. Ask them to write about any challenges they face and how they plan to overcome them. Regular journaling helps children develop self-awareness and strategic thinking skills by analyzing their progress and making adjustments as needed.[15]

- **Mind mapping.** Introduce children to mind mapping as a tool for organizing their thoughts and planning projects. Have them start with a central idea, such as a goal they want to achieve, and then branch out with related tasks, resources, and potential challenges. This visual approach to planning helps children see the connections between different elements of a plan and think strategically about how to move forward.[16]

These practices not only enhance your children's ability to think ahead and solve problems but also prepare them for success in all areas of life.

In the 2017 film *Spider-Man: Homecoming*, Peter Parker faces a formidable adversary, the Vulture, whose advanced technology far surpasses Peter's resources. Stripped of Tony Stark's high-tech suit, Peter must rely on his strategic thinking to dismantle the Vulture's illegal weapons operations. He carefully tracks the shipment routes, gathering intelligence and planning a way to stop the Vulture without relying on sophisticated gadgets. In the final battle, Peter strategically targets the Vulture's wings, understanding that disabling them will neutralize his enemy. This showcases Peter's ability to think ahead and remain composed under pressure, relying on his intellect and resourcefulness to overcome challenges.[17]

Strategic thinking helps your children anticipate challenges, identify opportunities, and make informed decisions. By developing this superpower, they learn to see beyond immediate circumstances and chart a course toward meaningful goals. Planning, adaptability, and problem-solving become second nature, allowing your children to navigate life's complexities with confidence. When they apply strategic thinking, they take control of their future rather than simply reacting to events. Whether setting personal goals, managing responsibilities, or solving problems, this skill empowers your children to act with purpose and direction. As your children strengthen this ability, they equip themselves to approach life with foresight and intention.

ACTION ITEMS

- Before you read further, take a few minutes to consider the information presented in this section.
- Imagine your children decades in the future (after many years of cultivating strategic thinking) and how they use this superpower to achieve their goals.
- Note how your children currently employ strategic thinking in their daily life. Take pride in the progress they've already achieved in developing this superpower.

- Evaluate the effectiveness of your current practices to help your children cultivate these skills.
- If you decide that your current efforts to help your children cultivate strategic thinking need to be improved, consider at least one improvement you can make in the coming weeks, months, or year.
- Develop a plan for implementing that improvement.

Now that we've addressed the superpower of strategic thinking, let's move on to resilience.

SUPERPOWER #7: RESILIENCE

Resilience is the ability to withstand and recover from adversity, challenges, or setbacks. It involves maintaining a steady mindset in the face of difficulties and adapting to changing circumstances without losing focus or motivation. This superpower enables you to navigate hardships with persistence and determination, allowing you to bounce back from failures or disappointments. Resilience is about staying mentally strong, maintaining emotional balance, and continuing to move forward despite obstacles. It requires flexibility, perseverance, and the ability to learn from tough experiences, ultimately allowing you to grow stronger and more capable in the process.[18]

As you nurture resilience in the young people in your life, you're teaching them one of the most valuable skills they can possess. Encourage them to see challenges as learning experiences, to stay flexible in their thinking, and to maintain hope and determination. By fostering the superpower of resilience, you're helping them become strong, adaptable individuals who can thrive in any situation life presents.

Training Missions for Children

Here are some activities children can engage in to cultivate resilience.

- **Overcoming challenges together.** Encourage children to take on challenges that require effort and persistence, such as completing a difficult puzzle, learning a new skill (such as preparing a healthy meal, drawing a complex scene, or coding a simple program), or tackling a school project. Support them through the process, reminding them that setbacks are a natural part of learning. Afterward, discuss what they learned and how they felt when they succeeded. This activity reinforces the idea that resilience is about not giving up, even when things get tough.[19]
- **Resilience role-playing.** Create role-playing scenarios where children can practice responding to challenging situations, such as losing a game, facing a disagreement with a friend, or handling a difficult task. Encourage them to think about how they can stay calm, find solutions, and keep trying even when things don't go as planned. Role-playing helps children prepare for real-life challenges by building their emotional resilience.[20]
- **Reflective storytelling.** Share stories with children about people who have shown resilience, whether from history, literature, or personal experience. After the story, discuss how the characters overcame their difficulties and what qualities helped them persevere. Ask children to share their own experiences of resilience and what they learned from those situations. Storytelling helps children connect with the concept of resilience and see its value in their own lives.[21]

- **Gratitude practice during tough times.** Teach children to focus on the positives even during challenging moments by practicing gratitude. Encourage them to think about things they are thankful for, even when they're feeling frustrated or upset. Keeping a gratitude journal or sharing gratitude during family meals can help shift their perspective and build emotional strength.[22]
- **Mindfulness and stress-relief techniques.** Introduce children to mindfulness practices, such as deep breathing, to help them manage stress and stay calm in difficult situations. Regular mindfulness practice can enhance their ability to cope with challenges by keeping their emotions in check and helping them approach problems with a clear mind.[23]
- **Setting and achieving small goals.** Help children set small, achievable goals that require effort and perseverance, such as improving a skill, completing a chore, or finishing a book. Celebrate their successes and discuss how they overcame any obstacles along the way. Setting and achieving goals builds confidence and shows children that they have the power to overcome challenges through persistence.[24]
- **Learning from mistakes.** When children make mistakes, guide them through reflecting on what happened and what they can learn from the experience. Encourage them to view mistakes as opportunities for growth rather than failures. This mindset helps children develop resilience by understanding that setbacks are a normal part of life and can lead to valuable lessons.[25]

These practices not only build emotional strength but also prepare your children to navigate life's ups and downs with confidence and determination.

In the 2019 film *Spider-Man: Far From Home*, Peter Parker feels overwhelmed and defeated after Mysterio manipulates him and reveals his true identity to the world. Despite his initial doubts, Peter bounces back, showing resilience by taking on Mysterio again. He learns from his previous failures, adapts his tactics, and ultimately defeats Mysterio in their second battle, reclaiming his role as Spider-Man. Peter's resilience shines through as he overcomes emotional and physical setbacks, rebuilds his confidence, and perseveres against a formidable enemy.[26]

Building the superpower of resilience in your children equips them to handle setbacks and challenges with a positive mindset. By guiding them to face difficulties, learn from failures, and persevere in the face of adversity, you help them develop the strength to bounce back from life's ups and downs. Resilience empowers your children to maintain focus and motivation even when things don't go as planned. As they nurture this superpower, your children will become more adaptable and confident in overcoming obstacles, preparing them to navigate the complexities of life with determination and grit.

ACTION ITEMS

- Before you read further, take a few minutes to consider the information presented in this section.
- Imagine your children decades in the future (after many years of cultivating resilience) and how they use this superpower to achieve their goals.
- Note how your children currently employ resilience in their daily life. Take pride in the progress they've already achieved in developing this superpower.

- Evaluate the effectiveness of your current practices to help your children cultivate these skills.
- If you decide that your current efforts to help your children cultivate resilience need to be improved, consider at least one improvement you can make in the coming weeks, months, or year.
- Develop a plan for implementing that improvement.

Now that we've addressed the strategic life skill of resilience, let's move on to creativity.

SUPERPOWER #8: CREATIVITY

Creativity is the ability to generate new ideas, think outside traditional parameters, and approach situations from fresh perspectives. It involves using imagination and originality to solve problems, express ideas, or create something innovative. This superpower allows you to explore different possibilities, make connections between seemingly unrelated concepts, and develop unique solutions. Creativity is not limited to artistic expression—it can be applied to various areas of life, from science and technology to everyday decision-making. It requires curiosity, openness, and a willingness to experiment with new approaches and ideas.[27]

Training Missions for Children

Here are some activities children can engage in to cultivate creativity.

- **Creative arts and crafts.** Set aside time for children to explore different art forms, such as painting, drawing, sculpting, or crafting. Provide a variety of materials and encourage them to create something entirely their own.

Don't focus on perfection—instead, emphasize the joy of expressing ideas through art. This activity allows children to explore their imagination and develop their artistic skills.[28]

- **Storytelling sessions.** Encourage children to create and tell their own stories. They can write them down, act them out, or even turn them into a short play with family or friends. Provide prompts to get them started, like "What if animals could talk?" or "Imagine a world made entirely of candy." Storytelling nurtures creativity by allowing children to invent worlds and characters that reflect their inner thoughts and dreams.[29]

- **DIY projects.** Involve children in do-it-yourself projects where they can design and build something from scratch. Whether it's making a birdhouse, creating a toy, or inventing a new game, these projects encourage hands-on creativity and problem-solving. Give them the freedom to experiment and learn from their mistakes, reinforcing the idea that creativity is about trying new things and thinking innovatively.[30]

- **Imaginative play.** Encourage children to engage in imaginative play, where they can invent scenarios, characters, and adventures. This could include playing dress-up, building a fort, or pretending to be explorers on a treasure hunt. Imaginative play allows children to stretch their creative muscles in a fun, unstructured way and fosters their ability to think creatively in everyday situations.[31]

- **Nature-inspired creations.** Take children outside to explore nature and gather inspiration for creative projects. They can collect leaves, rocks, or flowers to create natural art, or use the scenery as a backdrop for photography or painting. Nature is a rich source of inspiration that can spark creative ideas and help children connect with their environment in new ways.[32]

- **Creative problem-solving challenges.** Present children with creative challenges that require innovative thinking, such as building the tallest tower with limited materials, designing a new invention, or solving a mystery using clues. These challenges encourage them to think critically and use their creativity to find solutions, reinforcing the idea that creativity is not just about art but about approaching problems with a fresh perspective.[33]

By engaging in these activities, children can enhance their creative abilities and also prepare themselves to think creatively in all areas of life, making them more adaptable, resourceful, and open to new possibilities.

In the 2021 film *Spider-Man: No Way Home*, during the final battle against multiple villains from alternate universes, Peter Parker teams up with other versions of Spider-Man from different realities to creatively devise a solution. Instead of merely fighting the villains, Peter and his counterparts use their combined scientific knowledge and creativity to engineer antidotes that cure each villain, restoring them to their original forms. This innovative problem-solving approach allows Peter to resolve the conflict without resorting to unnecessary violence. Peter demonstrates his creativity and resourcefulness by choosing science over brute force, highlighting his ability to think beyond conventional tactics in high-stakes situations.[34]

Encouraging creativity in children empowers them to explore new ideas and break free from traditional ways of thinking. By fostering an environment where they feel free to express themselves, experiment with different approaches, and solve problems in innovative ways, you help them unlock their imaginative potential. Creativity enables your children to approach challenges with fresh perspectives and to find unique solutions. As they develop this superpower, your children will become more confident in their ability to innovate and bring their ideas to life, enriching their experiences and contributions in all areas of life.

ACTION ITEMS

- Before you read further, take a few minutes to consider the information presented in this section.
- Imagine your children decades in the future (after many years of cultivating creativity) and how they use this superpower to achieve their goals.
- Note how your children currently employ creativity in their daily life. Take pride in the progress they've already achieved in developing this superpower.
- Evaluate the effectiveness of your current practices to help your children cultivate these skills.
- If you decide that your current efforts to help your children cultivate creativity need to be improved, consider at least one improvement you can make in the coming weeks, months, or year.
- Develop a plan for implementing that improvement.

Let's circle back to Spider-Man, an emblematic figure whose story arcs within the pages of comic books illuminate a journey of self-development. Under the mask of Spider-Man, Peter Parker shows great commitment to personal responsibility, strategic thinking, resilience in the face of adversity, and an innovative spirit. As we venture beyond this chapter, let Spider-Man inspire us all to embrace these new superpowers on the path to becoming the hero of our own story.

Core personal development shapes how your children take ownership of their actions, plan for the future, and navigate challenges with confidence. When they embrace personal responsibility, they learn that their choices shape their lives. When they practice strategic thinking, they develop the ability to set goals and create a path forward. When they build resilience, they learn to adapt, persist, and grow from setbacks. And when they nurture creativity, they open themselves to new ideas and innovative solutions. By helping them strengthen these skills, you give them the tools to approach life with purpose, flexibility, and a mindset for growth.

In the next chapter, we'll explore how embracing analytical skills, critical thinking, problem-solving, and decision-making can further empower your children to become real-life superheroes.

3

ANALYTICAL AND DECISION-MAKING SKILLS

I n a world of opportunities and challenges, navigating complex situations with grace and foresight empowers you to excel in any endeavor you pursue. Here, we delve into the competencies that distinguish the good from the great—analytical skills, critical thinking, problem-solving, and decision-making skills.

An example of a superhero who demonstrates these skills is Iron Man,[1] whose strength lies in his suit and extraordinary ability to analyze complex situations and make critical decisions under pressure. His journey from a brilliant inventor to a heroic figure exemplifies how analytical and decision-making skills can create remarkable inventions and lives.[2]

As we explore these strategic life skills, keep in mind that each is interlinked, forming a synergistic framework that will propel you toward your ambitions and equip you to thrive in an ever-changing world. We'll start with the superpower of analytical skills.

SUPERPOWER #9: ANALYTICAL SKILLS

Analytical skills are the ability to methodically break down information, data, or problems into smaller parts to better understand and interpret them. This superpower involves recognizing patterns, identifying trends, and making connections between different pieces of information. It requires logical thinking, attention to detail, and the ability to organize complex information in a clear and manageable way. Mastering analytical skills means applying structured approaches to evaluating data, drawing conclusions, and making informed decisions based on thorough examination and reasoning.[3]

As you guide the young people in your life to develop their analytical skills, you're helping them become thoughtful, discerning individuals. Teach them to ask questions, seek out reliable information, and analyze situations before acting. By fostering the superpower of analytical skills, you're preparing them to make well-reasoned choices and to approach life's challenges with a clear, focused mind.

Training Missions for Children

Here are some activities children can engage in to cultivate analytical skills.

- **Puzzles and brain teasers.** Introduce children to brain teasers and puzzles, such as jigsaw puzzles, Sudoku, or crosswords that challenge them to think critically and analyze patterns. These activities help children develop logical thinking and problem-solving skills in a fun and engaging way.[4]

- **Science experiments.** Encourage children to conduct simple science experiments at home. Provide them with materials and guide them in forming hypotheses, conducting experiments, and analyzing the results. Discuss what they learned and how they arrived at their conclusions. This hands-on experience fosters curiosity and teaches children to think analytically about cause and effect.[5]

- **Strategy games.** Play strategy games like chess, checkers, or board games that require careful planning and decision-making. These games challenge children to think ahead, consider different possibilities, and make strategic choices based on their analysis of the situation. This activity enhances their ability to evaluate options and make logical decisions.[6]

- **Comparative analysis.** Encourage children to compare and contrast different items, ideas, or situations. For example, ask them to compare two books they've read, two animals, or two different historical events. Guide them in identifying similarities and differences and discussing why those differences might exist. Comparative analysis helps children sharpen their critical thinking and analytical skills.[7]

- **Data collection and interpretation.** Involve children in collecting data on something they're interested in, such as tracking weather patterns, recording daily activities, or measuring plant growth. After collecting the data, help them analyze it by looking for trends, making graphs, or drawing conclusions. This activity teaches children how to gather and interpret information systematically.[8]

- **Debate and discussion.** Hold friendly debates or discussions on topics of interest. Encourage children to research their viewpoints, present arguments, and consider counterarguments. After the debate, discuss the strengths and weaknesses of each side's arguments. This practice helps children develop the ability to analyze different perspectives and articulate their thoughts clearly.[9]

- **Story problem-solving.** Present children with story-based problems that require analytical thinking to solve. These could be real-life scenarios or fictional stories where they need to figure out a solution based on the information provided. Encourage them to break down the problem, identify key details, and consider multiple solutions before deciding on the best approach. These exercises strengthen children's analytical and reasoning skills.[10]

By engaging in these activities, children can not only enhance their ability to analyze situations but also prepare themselves to approach challenges with confidence and clarity, making them more capable and thoughtful individuals.

In the 2008 film *Iron Man*, after being captured by terrorists and ordered to build weapons, Tony Stark uses his sharp analytical skills to assess the materials available to him. Rather than constructing the missile he's been tasked with, Tony ingeniously designs and builds the first prototype of the Iron Man suit using only scrap parts. By carefully analyzing the functionality of each component and structure, he creates a highly advanced piece of technology from minimal resources. This situation underscores Tony's ability to break down complex problems into manageable parts, demonstrating his keen analytical mind and capacity to develop innovative solutions, even under extreme pressure.[11]

Fostering analytical skills in your children helps them develop the ability to break down complex problems and think logically about solutions. By encouraging them to ask questions, evaluate information, and consider different perspectives, you guide them toward making well-reasoned decisions. Analytical skills allow your children to approach challenges methodically, recognize patterns, and draw meaningful conclusions. As they cultivate this superpower, your children will be better equipped to navigate the complexities of life with clarity and sound judgment, enhancing their ability to succeed in various endeavors.

ACTION ITEMS

- Before you read further, take a few minutes to consider the information presented in this section.
- Imagine your children decades in the future (after many years of cultivating analytical skills) and how they use this superpower to achieve their goals.
- Note how your children currently employ analytical skills in their daily life. Take pride in the progress they've already achieved in developing this superpower.
- Evaluate the effectiveness of your current practices to help your children cultivate these skills.
- If you decide that your current efforts to help your children cultivate analytical skills need to be improved, consider at least one improvement you can make in the coming weeks, months, or year.
- Develop a plan for implementing that improvement.

Now that we've addressed analytical skills, let's move on to critical thinking and problem- solving.

SUPERPOWERS #10 & 11: CRITICAL THINKING AND PROBLEM-SOLVING SKILLS

Critical thinking and problem-solving are distinct superpowers, yet they share many similarities. The best way to understand them is through comparison. Let's start by defining and explaining each.

- *Critical thinking* is the ability to analyze information objectively, evaluate different perspectives, and draw well-reasoned conclusions. It's about questioning assumptions, examining evidence, and considering various viewpoints before making a decision. When individuals engage in critical thinking, they ask "why" and "how" about the information they receive. They actively challenge assumptions, weigh the evidence, and differentiate between opinion and fact. Critical thinkers also recognize biases—both their own and those of others. It's a reflective and structured approach to thinking, often involving steps like identifying the issue, analyzing the context, and seeking clarity.[12]
- *Problem-solving skills* refer to the ability to identify solutions to specific challenges or obstacles. It involves diagnosing the issue, brainstorming potential solutions, evaluating those solutions, and implementing the best one. In problem-solving, individuals are focused on fixing a situation that requires a clear, actionable response. Unlike critical thinking, which may involve broader, more abstract reasoning, problem-solving is goal-oriented and practical. It often requires creativity, logical thinking, and collaboration. Problem-solving can be more immediate, as it involves coming up with strategies that work in real time.[13]

Comparing Critical Thinking and Problem-Solving Skills

- **Focus.** Critical thinking emphasizes analyzing and evaluating information and ideas broadly, whereas problem-solving is more action-oriented, focusing on finding practical solutions to specific challenges.
- **Scope.** Critical thinking often deals with abstract, theoretical issues (e.g., evaluating arguments or evidence), while problem-solving is focused on concrete, real-world obstacles (e.g., logistical problems or interpersonal conflicts).
- **Process.** Both require analysis and evaluation, but critical thinking is more reflective, encouraging you to consider all sides of an issue, while problem-solving pushes you toward a solution, often through creative brainstorming and practical steps.
- **Benefits.** Critical thinking strengthens your ability to make sound judgments and learn, whereas problem-solving hones your ability to tackle challenges directly and efficiently.

Just as Iron Man questions assumptions and evaluates his options before making decisions in high-pressure situations, mastering critical thinking and problem-solving skills will empower you to approach issues logically and clearly.

Critical Thinking Training Missions for Children

Here are some activities children can engage in to cultivate this superpower.

- **Debate discussions.** Encourage children to engage in friendly debates on topics they find interesting, such as

"Which animal would make the best pet?" or "Should schools have longer recesses?" Guide them to research their position, consider counterarguments, and present their points clearly. After the debate, discuss the strengths and weaknesses of each argument. This activity helps children learn to evaluate different perspectives and articulate their thoughts.[14]

- **Question the story.** After reading a book or watching a movie, ask children to think critically about the plot, characters, and themes. Pose questions like, "Why do you think the character made that choice?" "What would have happened if the story had a different ending?" or "What message do you think the author was trying to convey?" This encourages children to dig deeper into the content and think critically about the narrative.[15]

- **Logic puzzles and games.** Introduce children to logic puzzles, riddles, and strategy games like Go, Minesweeper, or Zendo. These activities require them to think methodically, recognize patterns, and solve complex problems. Playing these games regularly sharpens their logical reasoning and enhances their critical thinking skills.[16]

- **Comparative analysis.** Choose two items, ideas, or situations for children to compare and contrast. For example, compare two different habitats, two historical events, or two methods of transportation. Encourage them to identify similarities, differences, and the implications of these differences. Comparative analysis helps children practice critical thinking by evaluating and contrasting different elements.[17]

- **"What if" scenarios.** Engage children in "what if" scenarios that require them to consider alternative outcomes or possibilities. Ask questions like, "What if humans could breathe underwater?" or "What if we didn't have to sleep?" Encourage them to explore the potential impacts of these hypothetical situations. This creative exercise helps them think outside established patterns and consider a range of possibilities.[18]

- **Evaluating sources.** Teach children how to critically evaluate the reliability of information sources, especially online. Show them how to check the credibility of an article, consider the author's intent, and recognize bias. Discuss the importance of questioning information and seeking evidence to support claims. This activity equips children with the skills to navigate information critically and responsibly.[19]

By engaging in these activities, children can enhance their ability to make informed decisions and prepare themselves to navigate the complexities of the world with confidence and clarity.

In the 2010 film *Iron Man 2*, Tony Stark is confronted with the life-threatening toxicity of his arc reactor, realizing that the palladium core is slowly poisoning him. Demonstrating his critical thinking skills, Tony revisits his father's research and uncovers clues that point to the creation of a new, sustainable element. By synthesizing this element, Tony successfully solves the reactor issue and saves his own life. His ability to question assumptions, delve into the scientific details, and apply his knowledge exemplifies his critical thinking, enabling him to develop a groundbreaking solution in a life-or-death situation.[20]

Problem-Solving Training Missions for Children

Here are some activities children can engage in to cultivate this superpower.

- **Puzzle challenges.** Introduce children to a variety of puzzles, such as jigsaw puzzles, logic puzzles, or Rubik's Cubes. Encourage them to approach the puzzle methodically, considering different strategies and experimenting with solutions until they succeed. This activity sharpens their problem-solving abilities and teaches patience and perseverance.[21]
- **Creative building projects.** Provide children with building materials like LEGO bricks, blocks, or recycled materials, and challenge them to construct something specific, such as a bridge, tower, or vehicle. Encourage them to think about the design, stability, and functionality of their creation. Building projects help children develop spatial reasoning and problem-solving skills as they figure out how to bring their ideas to life.[22]
- **Mystery scenarios.** Present children with mystery scenarios that require them to solve a problem or figure out a puzzle. For example, create a treasure hunt with clues that lead to a hidden prize or set up a "whodunit" mystery where they must gather clues and identify the culprit. These scenarios engage children in critical thinking and encourage them to use logic and deduction.[23]
- **Brainstorming sessions.** When faced with a challenge, encourage children to brainstorm multiple solutions. Create a list of possible approaches, no matter how unconventional, and then discuss the pros and cons of each option. This activity teaches children that there are

often many ways to solve a problem and that thinking creatively can lead to effective solutions.[24]

- **Role-playing problem-solving.** Engage in role-playing activities where children act out real-life situations that require problem-solving. For instance, they might role-play resolving a conflict with a friend, finding a lost item, or planning a school project. Afterward, discuss the strategies they used and how they might improve their approach in the future. Role-playing helps children practice problem-solving in a safe and supportive environment.[25]
- **Science and engineering challenges.** Organize science or engineering challenges where children must build a structure, create a functioning model, or design an experiment to achieve a specific goal. These challenges encourage them to apply scientific principles, test their ideas, and refine their solutions through trial and error. This hands-on experience reinforces the importance of persistence and adaptability in problem-solving.[26]
- **Daily problem-solving practice.** Incorporate problem-solving into daily routines by encouraging children to take an active role in resolving everyday issues. This could include figuring out how to organize their room, deciding what to do if they miss the bus, or finding a way to share a toy with a sibling. These real-life situations provide valuable opportunities for children to practice and refine their problem-solving skills.[27]

By engaging in these activities, children can develop the super-power of problem-solving skills, learning to approach challenges with a thoughtful and systematic mindset and preparing them to tackle any obstacle they encounter in life.

In the 2013 film *Iron Man 3*, Tony Stark is left stranded without access to his usual advanced technology after the Mandarin forces destroy his home. Forced to rely on basic tools, Tony demonstrates his ingenuity by crafting makeshift gadgets to infiltrate the enemy's hideout and continue his mission. His quick thinking and ability to adapt under pressure highlight his remarkable resourcefulness. This situation exemplifies Tony's problem-solving skills, as he devises creative solutions in the face of adversity, using innovation and sharp instincts to overcome unexpected challenges.[28]

Cultivating critical thinking and problem-solving skills in your children equips them to face challenges with a proactive and resourceful approach. By guiding them to identify issues, brainstorm potential solutions, and evaluate outcomes, you help them develop the ability to tackle obstacles effectively. Critical thinking and problem-solving skills enable your children to approach difficulties confidently and persistently, finding ways to overcome hurdles and achieve their goals. As they develop this superpower, your children will become more adept at navigating life's complexities, turning challenges into opportunities for growth and learning.

ACTION ITEMS

- Before you read further, take a few minutes to consider the information presented in this section.
- Imagine your children decades in the future (after many years of cultivating critical thinking and problem-solving skills) and how they use these superpowers to achieve their goals.

- Note how your children currently employ critical thinking and problem-solving skills in their daily life. Take pride in the progress they've already achieved in developing these superpowers.
- Evaluate the effectiveness of your current practices to help your children cultivate these skills.
- If you decide that your current efforts to help your children cultivate critical thinking and problem-solving skills need to be improved, consider at least one improvement you can make in the coming weeks, months, or year.
- Develop a plan for implementing that improvement.

Now that we've addressed the superpowers of critical thinking and problem-solving skills, let's move on to decision-making skills.

SUPERPOWER #12: DECISION-MAKING SKILLS

Decision-making skills are the ability to evaluate different options, assess potential outcomes, and choose the most effective course of action. This superpower involves a process of gathering information, analyzing facts, and considering various perspectives before reaching a conclusion. It requires thinking critically, weighing pros and cons, and making choices with clarity and confidence, even when faced with uncertainty or pressure. Mastering decision-making skills means developing a systematic approach to making thoughtful, informed decisions in various situations, from daily life choices to more complex and challenging situations.[29]

As you guide the young people in your life to develop their decision-making skills, you're helping them become thoughtful, deliberate individuals who are capable of making choices that reflect their best interests. Encourage them to gather information, evaluate their options carefully, and trust in their judgment. By fostering the superpower of decision-making, you're preparing them to take control of their lives and to make decisions that lead to positive, meaningful outcomes.

The Nexus Between Superpowers

You've likely noticed that all the superpowers discussed in this chapter equip you to make better decisions. Skills like analytical thinking, critical thinking, and problem-solving offer valuable insights that guide your choices. In the previous chapter, we explored how strategic thinking forms the foundation for making strategic decisions. More broadly, every superpower in this book —from stress management to learning skills—relies on the ability to make informed decisions. In each instance, information must be carefully assessed before reaching a conclusion.

It's appropriate to view decision-making as the nexus, or the common thread, connecting all the superpowers. At the core of wielding any superpower is the ability to gather and assess information before deciding on a course of action. While each life skill plays a role in personal development, decision-making is the most crucial. Ultimately, our lives can be seen as the sum of our decisions. Mastering the superpower of decision-making empowers us to navigate life's challenges with precision and care.

Ethical Decisions

Ethical decision-making involves making choices that align with moral principles and contribute positively to the well-being of others and society. Recognize when choices have moral implications. Ethical values affecting decision-making include trustworthiness, respect, responsibility, fairness, caring, and citizenship. Evaluate how decisions affect you, others, your community, and your nation. By consistently practicing ethical decision-making, you build a foundation of integrity and trust, guiding your actions to positively impact your life and those around you.[30]

Iron Man's internal conflict about the ethics of his technology shows how critical it is to evaluate not just what you *can* do, but what you *should* do. Ethical decision-making ensures that your actions reflect your values and contribute to a better world.

Training Missions for Children

Here are some activities children can engage in to cultivate decision-making skills.

- **Pros and cons lists.** Teach children to make pros and cons lists when faced with a decision. Whether it's choosing what to do on the weekend, selecting a book to read, or deciding how to spend their allowance, guide them in listing the advantages and disadvantages of each option. This method helps them visualize the potential impact of their choices and supports more balanced decision-making.[31]
- **Real-life choices.** Give children opportunities to make real-life decisions that affect them, such as choosing their own clothes, planning a small budget, or deciding how to organize their study time. Allow them to experience the consequences of their choices, whether positive or negative, and discuss what they learned from the experience. Real-life decision-making builds confidence and accountability.[32]

- **Decision-making scenarios.** Present children with hypothetical scenarios that require them to make a decision. For example, ask them how they would choose between two after-school activities, what they would do if they found money on the ground, or how they would handle a disagreement with a friend. Encourage them to think about the potential outcomes of each choice and discuss their reasoning. This activity helps children practice weighing options and considering consequences.[33]
- **Role-playing decision-making.** Engage children in role-playing activities where they must make decisions in various scenarios. For example, they could role-play being a store owner deciding what to stock, a teacher deciding how to handle a classroom situation, or a leader making a choice for their team. After the role-play, discuss the decisions they made and what influenced their choices. Role-playing allows children to explore decision-making in a safe and supportive environment.[34]
- **Group decision-making exercises.** Involve children in group decision-making activities, such as planning a family outing, organizing a small event, or deciding on a group project. Encourage them to collaborate, listen to each other's ideas, and work together to reach a consensus. This activity teaches them the value of considering multiple perspectives and making decisions that benefit the group.[35]
- **Discussing ethical dilemmas.** Introduce children to simple ethical dilemmas that require careful consideration of values and consequences. For example, discuss situations like whether it's okay to keep a secret if it might hurt someone, or what they would do if they saw someone being treated unfairly. Encourage them to think about

their values and how those values influence their decisions. This activity helps children develop moral reasoning and ethical decision-making skills.[36]

- **Decision-making journal.** Encourage children to keep a journal where they record important decisions they've made, along with the thought process and outcome. They can reflect on what they learned from each decision and how they might approach similar situations in the future. This practice helps children become more aware of their decision-making patterns and fosters continuous improvement.[37]

By engaging in these activities, children can enhance their ability to make thoughtful decisions and prepare themselves to navigate life's challenges with responsibility and integrity.

In the 2019 film *Avengers: Endgame*, Tony Stark's decision to wield the Infinity Gauntlet and snap Thanos and his army out of existence exemplifies the gravity of his decision-making skills. Aware that using the Gauntlet will cost him his life, Tony chooses to act, fully understanding that it is the only way to save the universe. This moment underscores his ability to make high-stakes decisions while considering the immense consequences. Tony's choice reflects his capacity to weigh risks and benefits, ultimately sacrificing himself for the greater good and taking full responsibility for the outcome.[38]

Teaching decision-making skills to your children helps them learn how to evaluate options, consider consequences, and make choices with confidence. By guiding them through the process of weighing pros and cons and reflecting on the outcomes of their decisions, you empower them to take responsibility for their choices.

Decision-making skills enable your children to navigate life's challenges with a clear and thoughtful approach, helping them to achieve their goals and learn from their experiences. As they strengthen this superpower, your children will become more capable of making sound decisions that lead to positive outcomes in their personal and academic lives.

ACTION ITEMS

- Before you read further, take a few minutes to consider the information presented in this section.
- Imagine your children decades in the future (after many years of cultivating decision-making skills) and how they use this superpower to achieve their goals.
- Note how your children currently employ decision-making skills in their daily life. Take pride in the progress they've already achieved in developing this superpower.
- Evaluate the effectiveness of your current practices to cultivate your children's decision-making skills.
- If you decide that your current efforts to cultivate this superpower need to be improved, consider at least one improvement you can make in the coming weeks, months, or year.
- Develop a plan for implementing that improvement.

As we close this chapter on analytical and decision-making skills, it's fitting to return to the inspiring example of Iron Man. His transformation from a gifted inventor to a globally recognized superhero underscores the impact that analytical and decision-making skills can have. Tony Stark's ability to confront challenges, both in his personal life and on the battlefield, with a calm, calculated approach is a testament to the power of these skills. Just as Iron Man assembles his suit piece by piece, your children can build their future with the same deliberate and thoughtful strategies.

Analytical and decision-making skills shape how your children approach challenges, evaluate information, and make thoughtful choices. When they develop analytical skills, they learn to break down complex situations and recognize patterns. When they practice critical thinking and problem-solving, they question assumptions, explore different perspectives, and find effective solutions. When they strengthen decision-making skills, they weigh options, consider consequences, and take action with confidence. These abilities help them navigate school, work, and life with clarity and purpose. By encouraging these skills, you prepare them to think independently, adapt to new situations, and make choices that align with their values and goals.

In the next chapter, we'll explore how embracing communication skills, interpersonal skills, negotiating skills, and conflict resolution can further empower your children to become real-life superheroes.

RAISING A GENERATION OF SUPERHEROS

"Superheroes are the best of us. Never mind all those powers or the crazy costumes. The heart of a superhero is meant to inspire."

— MARJORIE LIU

This book's superpower theme came about partly because we're talking about children, and all kids love a good superhero. But there's much more to it than that. I really do think life skills are the superpowers of the real world, yet they're so often overlooked in a child's education. This isn't your fault as a parent; it happens because there's so much pressure on us to teach them other things. The focus at school is academic, and their time is stretched thinly between homework and after-school activities. There's not much time for anyone to teach them anything else. I hope that you're finding the training missions throughout this book easy to fit in with all the other things you're trying to balance and that you're beginning to see some of those superpowers start to develop.

What we're trying to do here is infuse our children with confidence and resilience and show them how to be kind, responsible humans with drive and purpose. This is a character profile that could be applied to just about any superhero you can think of. Think about it. They're strong, kind, honorable, and confident, and they have a clear purpose with every mission they take on. This is something every person is able to embody when they have the right training. I would have loved guidance like this when my children were younger, and now that I've watched them grow up and raise children of their own, I see it almost as a calling to be part of a movement that teaches these skills to the younger generation.

Children are under so much more pressure now than they were when you and I were their age, and many of them face challenges with their mental health as a result of this. Having life's super-powers in their toolkit as early as possible is going to help them avoid this fate. If this idea moves you as much as it does me, please take a moment to help me reach more families by leaving a short review of this book.

By leaving a review of this book on Amazon, you'll make it easier for new readers to find it, and you'll show them a clear blueprint that they can use to boost their child's superpowers.

Parents realize there's a need to teach their children the important life skills they're not being taught in school, and they're searching for guidance. Your review will help them find it and see that this is something they can do much more easily than they thought.

Thank you so much for your support. Together, we can raise a whole generation of superheroes.

Scan the QR code below.

[QR code]

4

COMMUNICATION AND INTERPERSONAL SKILLS

Consider Wonder Woman (Diana Prince), who exemplifies powerful communication and interpersonal skills through her diplomatic nature, empathy, and ability to unite people from different backgrounds. As an ambassador for peace, Wonder Woman consistently resolves conflicts through strength, negotiation, understanding, and compassion. Her leadership style is rooted in her ability to connect with people personally, inspiring trust and collaboration.

Four pivotal skills—communication, interpersonal, negotiating, and conflict resolution—are at the heart of this chapter. We'll start with communication skills.

SUPERPOWER #13: COMMUNICATION SKILLS

Communication skills are the ability to clearly and effectively convey ideas, thoughts, and information to others. This superpower involves not only speaking or writing with clarity but also actively listening, interpreting nonverbal cues, and adapting your message to different audiences. It requires the ability to express oneself confidently while ensuring that the intended message is understood by the recipient. Mastering communication skills means being aware of tone, context, and audience needs, and using various mediums—such as verbal, written, or digital communication—appropriately and effectively.[1]

Wonder Woman's ability to express her ideas with clarity and conviction, whether she's speaking to world leaders or calming a tense situation, showcases the power of clear communication in building trust and resolving conflicts.

As you nurture communication skills in the young people in your life, you're teaching them to express themselves confidently and empathetically. Encourage them to listen actively, to speak with clarity and purpose, and to be mindful of how their words and actions affect others. By fostering the superpower of communication, you're equipping them to build strong, healthy relationships and to navigate the world with confidence and compassion.

Training Missions for Children

Here are some activities children can engage in to cultivate communication skills.

- **Storytelling practice.** Encourage children to share stories about their day, a favorite memory, or something they've imagined. Give them the floor during family meals or before bedtime, and then ask questions to help them elaborate on their story. This activity helps children practice organizing their thoughts, speaking confidently, and engaging their audience.[2]
- **Active listening games.** Play games that focus on active listening, such as "Telephone" or "Simon Says." After the

game, discuss the importance of paying attention to what others are saying and how it helps avoid misunderstandings. These games teach children the value of listening carefully and responding appropriately.[3]

- **Role-playing conversations.** Set up role-playing scenarios where children can practice different types of communication, such as asking for help, expressing feelings, or resolving a conflict. For example, they might role-play asking a teacher for clarification on an assignment or telling a friend how they feel about something. Afterward, discuss how they handled the conversation and what they could improve. Role-playing helps children build confidence in communicating in various situations.[4]

- **Letter writing.** Encourage children to write letters to friends, family members, or even fictional characters. This could be a thank-you note, an invitation, or a letter expressing their feelings. Writing letters helps children practice organizing their thoughts and expressing themselves clearly in writing, which is an important aspect of communication.[5]

- **Group discussions.** Involve children in group discussions on topics they care about, such as a recent book they've read, a family outing, or a current event. Encourage them to share their opinions, listen to others, and build on each other's ideas. Group discussions teach children how to articulate their thoughts, respect differing viewpoints, and engage in meaningful conversations.[6]

- **Nonverbal communication awareness.** Teach children about the importance of nonverbal communication, such as body language, facial expressions, and tone of voice. Play charades or other games where they have to communicate without words, and then discuss how these nonverbal cues can convey feelings and intentions. Understanding nonverbal communication helps children become more effective communicators.[7]

- **Feedback practice.** Help children learn how to give and receive constructive feedback. Encourage them to share their thoughts on a sibling's drawing, a friend's story, or a family project, focusing on both positive aspects and areas for improvement. Teach them how to receive feedback graciously and use it to grow. This practice fosters open, respectful communication and helps children improve their communication skills.[8]

By practicing these skills, children not only strengthen their ability to communicate effectively but also develop the empathy, respect, and confidence needed to engage with others throughout their lives.

In the 2017 film *Wonder Woman*, Diana Prince exemplifies strong communication skills when she makes the bold decision to cross No Man's Land, despite the advice of others. Her conversation with Steve Trevor and the team is both clear and decisive. Diana passionately articulates her reasoning, not only leading through her actions but also by expressing her values and intentions with conviction. This direct communication inspires those around her to rally in support, ultimately leading to a crucial breakthrough on the battlefield. In this scene, Wonder Woman embodies assertiveness, clarity, and conviction—essential qualities for leadership and persuading others to follow.[9]

Developing communication skills in your children equips them to express their thoughts clearly, listen effectively, and engage with others in meaningful ways. By encouraging them to articulate their ideas, ask questions, and listen with empathy, you help them build strong connections with others. Communication skills enable your children to navigate social situations, resolve conflicts, and collaborate with others. As they develop this superpower, your children will be better prepared to interact confidently and effectively, fostering positive relationships and achieving success in both personal and academic settings.

ACTION ITEMS

- Before you read further, take a few minutes to consider the information presented in this section.
- Imagine your children decades in the future (after many years of cultivating communication skills) and how they use this superpower to achieve their goals.
- Note how your children currently employ communication skills in their daily life. Take pride in the progress they've already achieved in developing this superpower.
- Evaluate the effectiveness of your current practices to help your children cultivate these skills.
- If you decide that your current efforts to help your children cultivate communication skills need to be improved, consider at least one improvement you can make in the coming weeks, months, or year.
- Develop a plan for implementing that improvement.

Now that we've addressed the superpower of communication skills, let's move on to interpersonal skills.

SUPERPOWER #14: INTERPERSONAL SKILLS

Interpersonal skills are the ability to interact effectively and harmoniously with others. This superpower involves understanding social dynamics, being aware of others' emotions and perspectives, and communicating in ways that foster positive relationships. It requires empathy, respect, and trust. Mastering interpersonal skills means navigating social situations with ease, adjusting to different personalities, and building strong connections through effective, meaningful interactions.[10]

As you guide the young people in your life to develop their interpersonal skills, you're helping them become socially aware, emotionally intelligent individuals who can thrive in any environment. Encourage them to practice empathy, to be considerate of others' perspectives, and to engage in active, respectful communication. By fostering the superpower of interpersonal skills, you're equipping them to build strong, lasting relationships and to contribute positively to their communities and beyond.

Empathy, Respect, and Trust

At the core of interpersonal skills are three elements.[11]

- **Empathy.** Understanding and sharing another person's feelings creates genuine connections and deepens communication.[12]
- **Respect.** Recognizing everyone's inherent value fosters mutual appreciation, understanding, and constructive conflict resolution.[13]
- **Trust.** Built through consistent actions and integrity, trust allows for open ideas, risk-taking, and collaboration in a safe environment.[14]

Wonder Woman's empathy for others, whether comforting those in distress or mediating conflicts, shows that understanding another person's perspective is key to building meaningful, lasting connections. Empathy often serves as the foundational element, leading to respect and trust. These three elements uplift your interpersonal effectiveness, making you a better friend, collaborator, and leader.

Training Missions for Children

Here are some activities children can engage in to cultivate interpersonal skills.

- **Empathy exercises.** Help children develop empathy by engaging in activities that encourage them to understand and appreciate other people's feelings and perspectives. For example, read a story together and discuss how the characters might feel in different situations. Ask questions like, "How would you feel if you were in their shoes?" or "What do you think they need right now?" These exercises help children practice seeing the world from another person's point of view.[15]
- **Social etiquette practice.** Teach children the basics of social etiquette, such as greeting others politely, saying "please" and "thank you," and taking turns in conversations. Practice these skills through games or by role-playing different social situations, such as meeting someone new or attending a family gathering. Understanding social etiquette helps children feel more confident and comfortable in social interactions.[16]
- **Compliment circle.** Organize a compliment circle where each child gives a sincere compliment to another. This could be done in a family setting, classroom, or among friends. Encourage them to think about what they genuinely appreciate about the other person. This activity fosters a positive atmosphere, strengthens bonds, and

helps children understand the importance of kindness and encouragement in relationships.[17]

- **Listening and reflecting.** Teach children the importance of active listening by engaging in listening and reflecting exercises. Pair up children and have one talk about a topic while the other listens carefully. The listener then reflects back what they heard, focusing on understanding and empathy. This practice helps children develop the skill of truly listening to others, which is key to strong interpersonal relationships.[18]

By engaging in these practices, children enhance their ability to interact effectively with others and to navigate social situations with empathy, respect, and confidence throughout their lives.

In the 2017 film *Wonder Woman*, Diana Prince exemplified interpersonal skills through her interactions with Steve Trevor's team, which includes characters like Charlie, Sameer, and The Chief. Despite coming from a background vastly different from theirs, Diana connects with each of them on a personal level. She listens with empathy, offers encouragement, and shows genuine interest in their stories, which helps her build trust and camaraderie. This ability to understand and relate to others' emotions and experiences is key to fostering strong relationships and is essential for teamwork and cooperation.[19]

Helping your children develop interpersonal skills allows them to build and maintain positive relationships with others. You guide them in forming meaningful connections by teaching them to understand and respect different perspectives, communicate effectively, and collaborate with peers. Interpersonal skills enable your children to work well with others, resolve conflicts, and contribute to a supportive community. As they develop this superpower, your children will be better equipped to navigate social interactions and build strong, healthy relationships throughout their life.

ACTION ITEMS

- Before you read further, take a few minutes to consider the information presented in this section.
- Imagine your children decades in the future (after many years of cultivating interpersonal skills) and how they use this superpower to achieve their goals.
- Note how your children currently employ interpersonal skills in their daily life. Take pride in the progress they've already achieved in developing this superpower.
- Evaluate the effectiveness of your current practices to help your children cultivate these skills.
- If you decide that your current efforts to help your children cultivate interpersonal skills need to be improved, consider at least one improvement you can make in the coming weeks, months, or year.
- Develop a plan for implementing that improvement.

Now that we've addressed the superpower of interpersonal skills, let's move on to negotiating skills.

SUPERPOWER #15: NEGOTIATING SKILLS

Negotiating skills are the ability to engage in discussions to reach an agreement or compromise between two or more parties. This superpower involves understanding both sides' needs, desires, and goals while effectively communicating your own. It requires preparation, active listening, and the capacity to find common ground by proposing solutions that address all parties' interests.

Mastering negotiating skills means navigating complex situations with tact, flexibility, and a focus on achieving mutually beneficial outcomes.[20]

Wonder Woman often uses her negotiating prowess to unite opposing sides in diplomatic talks or during conflicts.

As you help the young people in your life develop their negotiating skills, you're equipping them to handle conflicts and opportunities with grace and assertiveness. Encourage them to listen actively, to articulate their needs and desires, and to approach negotiations with an open mind. By fostering the superpower of negotiating skills, you're preparing them to advocate for themselves and others, to find solutions in difficult situations, and to achieve outcomes that are fair and balanced.

Training Missions for Children

Here are some activities children can engage in to cultivate negotiating skills.

- **Role-playing negotiations.** Set up role-playing scenarios where children practice negotiating in everyday situations, such as deciding on which game to play, dividing chores with siblings, or choosing a movie for family night. Encourage them to listen to each other's viewpoints, propose compromises, and work toward a mutually agreeable solution. This activity helps children understand the give-and-take involved in successful negotiations.[21]
- **Mock marketplace.** Create a mock marketplace where children can buy, sell, or trade items with each other using pretend money or tokens. Encourage them to negotiate prices, terms, and deals with one another. This exercise teaches children the basics of bargaining, how to advocate

for what they want, and the importance of fairness in transactions.[22]

- **Family decision-making.** Involve children in family decisions where negotiations are needed, such as planning a vacation, deciding on a weekend activity, or setting house rules. Allow them to voice their opinions, propose compromises, and help reach a consensus. This practice shows children that their opinions are valued and that negotiation is a collaborative process.[23]

- **Negotiation games.** Play games that involve negotiation, such as Monopoly, Settlers of Catan, or card games where trades and deals are part of the strategy. These games offer a fun way for children to practice negotiating while also teaching them to think strategically and consider the long-term consequences of their decisions.[24]

- **Understanding needs and wants.** Teach children the difference between needs and wants by discussing scenarios where they must prioritize one over the other. For example, talk about how to decide between saving money for something important versus spending it on a treat. This helps children develop the ability to negotiate based on what truly matters and to recognize when a compromise is necessary.[25]

- **Reflective journaling on negotiations.** Encourage children to keep a journal where they reflect on any negotiations they've been involved in, whether at home, school, or in social settings. Have them write about what worked, what didn't, and what they learned from the experience. This reflective practice helps them improve their negotiating skills over time and become more aware of their own negotiation style.[26]

- **Problem-solving discussions.** When conflicts arise among siblings or friends, guide children through a structured problem-solving discussion where they negotiate a solution. Encourage them to express their needs, listen to the other person's perspective, and brainstorm possible solutions together. This approach fosters a deeper understanding of negotiation as a tool for conflict resolution.[27]

These practices enhance children's ability to advocate for themselves and prepare them to navigate relationships and challenges with confidence and empathy throughout their lives.

In the 2017 film *Wonder Woman*, Diana Prince showcases her negotiating skills during her confrontation with the British War Council. Though initially dismissed, she challenges their war strategy, advocating for a moral approach rather than simply accepting their tactics. Her persistence and unwavering commitment to doing what's right— insisting they cannot stand idly by while people suffer— ultimately make an impact. Diana's firm stance inspires Steve Trevor to act, illustrating that negotiation isn't always about compromise. Sometimes, it's about holding fast to your values while persuading others to recognize a broader, more ethical perspective.[28]

Teaching your children negotiating skills helps them learn how to advocate for themselves while considering the needs and perspectives of others. By guiding them to find common ground, make compromises, and seek win-win solutions, you prepare them to handle conflicts and reach agreements effectively. Negotiating skills enable your children to navigate social and professional interactions with confidence and fairness. As they develop this superpower, your children will be better equipped to achieve balanced outcomes in various situations, fostering positive relationships and ensuring their voice is heard.

ACTION ITEMS

- Before you read further, take a few minutes to consider the information presented in this section.
- Imagine your children decades in the future (after many years of cultivating negotiating skills) and how they use this superpower to achieve their goals.
- Note how your children currently employ negotiating skills in their daily life. Take pride in the progress they've already achieved in developing this superpower.
- Evaluate the effectiveness of your current practices to help your children cultivate these skills.
- If you decide that your current efforts to help your children cultivate negotiating skills need to be improved, consider at least one improvement you can make in the coming weeks, months, or year.
- Develop a plan for implementing that improvement.

Now that we've addressed the superpower of negotiating skills, let's move on to conflict resolution.

SUPERPOWER #16: CONFLICT RESOLUTION

Conflict resolution is the ability to constructively navigate and address disagreements or disputes between individuals or groups. This superpower involves identifying the root causes of conflicts, understanding the perspectives of all parties involved, and facilitating open, respectful communication to find a solution. It requires patience, empathy, and the skill to de-escalate tense situations while guiding others toward a common understanding or agreement. Mastering conflict resolution means mediating differences effectively and promoting harmony through collaborative problem-solving.[29]

Wonder Woman's ability to mediate conflicts with strength and compassion exemplifies how resolving disputes with empathy can create lasting peace and understanding.

As you guide the young people in your life to develop their conflict resolution skills, you're teaching them to approach conflicts with empathy, patience, and a focus on finding mutually beneficial solutions. Encourage them to remain calm under pressure, to seek to understand before being understood, and to collaborate on resolving differences. By fostering the superpower of conflict resolution, you're equipping them to handle life's inevitable disagreements with confidence, fairness, and compassion, paving the way for healthier, more harmonious relationships.

Training Missions for Children

Here are some activities children can engage in to cultivate conflict resolution.

- **Conflict role-playing.** Set up role-playing scenarios where children practice resolving conflicts in a variety of situations, such as sharing toys, deciding on a game, or handling a misunderstanding with a friend. Encourage them to express their feelings calmly, listen to the other person's perspective, and work together to find a solution that everyone agrees on. Role-playing helps children build confidence in their ability to handle real-life conflicts effectively.[30]
- **The "I" statement practice.** Teach children how to use "I" statements to express their feelings without blaming

others, such as "I feel upset when you take my things without asking." Practice this technique in different scenarios so they can learn to communicate their emotions clearly and constructively. Using "I" statements helps reduce defensiveness and opens the door to more productive conversations.[31]

- **Conflict resolution circle.** When a conflict arises between siblings or friends, guide them in creating a conflict resolution circle. Each person takes turns expressing their perspective while the others listen without interrupting. After everyone has spoken, work together to brainstorm solutions that address everyone's concerns. This activity fosters a sense of fairness and collaboration in resolving disagreements.[32]

- **Problem-solving steps.** Teach children a simple, step-by-step approach to resolving conflicts: 1) Identify the problem, 2) Listen to each other's perspectives, 3) Brainstorm solutions, 4) Agree on a solution, and 5) Reflect on how it worked. Practice this method during conflicts at home or in group activities. Following a structured process helps children approach conflicts calmly and logically.[33]

- **Peace-making projects.** Encourage children to participate in projects that promote peace and understanding, such as creating "peace posters" or writing stories about resolving conflicts peacefully. These creative activities help reinforce the importance of empathy, kindness, and finding peaceful solutions in everyday life.[34]

- **Mediation practice.** Involve children in mediating conflicts between others, such as helping younger siblings or friends resolve a disagreement. Guide them in listening to both sides, asking open-ended questions, and suggesting fair solutions. Mediation practice helps children develop leadership skills and reinforces the idea that conflicts can be resolved without escalation.[35]

- **Reflection journaling.** Encourage children to keep a reflection journal where they write about any conflicts they experience and how they handled them. Have them reflect on what they did well, what they could improve, and what they learned from the situation. Reflective journaling helps children gain insight into their conflict resolution skills and fosters personal growth.[36]

These practices enhance your children's ability to navigate social situations and prepare them to build healthy, respectful relationships throughout their lives.

> In the 2017 film *Wonder Woman,* Diana Prince demonstrates her conflict resolution skills during her battle with Ares. She faces not only a physical clash but a profound moral dilemma. Ares attempts to persuade her that humanity is inherently evil and deserves destruction. Rather than simply engaging in combat, Diana reflects on her own experiences with people, ultimately resolving the conflict within herself. She chooses love and compassion over vengeance, reaffirming her belief in humanity's potential for good. This decision not only resolves the immediate conflict but also solidifies her guiding principle that true conflict resolution involves more than external battles—it requires inner clarity, staying true to one's values, and choosing a path that fosters peace and understanding.[37]

Helping your children develop conflict resolution skills equips them to manage disagreements and differences with understanding and respect. By teaching them to listen actively, communicate their feelings, and seek mutually beneficial solutions, you guide them in resolving conflicts constructively. Conflict resolution skills enable your children to navigate challenging situations with empathy and fairness, fostering positive relationships and reducing tension. As they cultivate this superpower, your children will be better prepared to handle conflicts in a way that promotes harmony and cooperation in their interactions with others.

ACTION ITEMS

- Before you read further, take a few minutes to consider the information presented in this section.
- Imagine your children decades in the future (after many years of cultivating conflict-resolution skills) and how they use this superpower to achieve their goals.
- Note how your children currently employ conflict-resolution skills in their daily life. Take pride in the progress they've already achieved in developing this superpower.
- Evaluate the effectiveness of your current practices to help your children cultivate these skills.
- If you decide that your current efforts to help your children cultivate conflict-resolution skills need to be improved, consider at least one improvement you can make in the coming weeks, months, or year.
- Develop a plan for implementing that improvement.

As we conclude this chapter on communication and interpersonal skills, let's revisit the inspiring example of Wonder Woman. She teaches us the profound impact of skilled communication, empathy, and understanding in leading and uniting individuals from diverse backgrounds. Just as Wonder Woman leverages her gifts for the greater good, so can we harness our communication and interpersonal skills to lead with empathy, respect, and trust, transforming challenges into opportunities for growth and unity.

Mastering communication and interpersonal skills empowers your children to express themselves clearly, understand others, and build meaningful relationships. When they practice active listening, they strengthen connections. When they negotiate effectively, they find solutions that respect different perspectives. When they resolve conflicts with patience and understanding, they create harmony in their interactions. These skills shape how they collaborate, lead, and navigate the world. By fostering these abilities, you help your children develop confidence in their voice, respect for others, and the tools to engage with people in positive and productive ways.

In the next chapter, we'll explore how embracing leadership, emotional intelligence, teamwork, and responsible citizenship can further empower your children to become real-life superheroes.

5

LEADERSHIP AND TEAMWORK

L eadership and teamwork are the superpowers that, when mastered, can transform your dreams into reality.

Drawing inspiration from Captain America, a leadership figure within the Marvel Universe, we can extract valuable lessons.[1] His exemplary attributes—from emotional intelligence and the ability to blend with diverse personalities to his unwavering commitment and sense of duty—serve as an example for aspiring leaders, demonstrating that effective leadership surpasses the boundaries of age and formal titles.[2]

In this chapter, we'll delve into the strategic life skills of leadership, emotional intelligence, teamwork, and responsible citizenship, each an essential component in a young visionary's toolbox. We'll begin with leadership skills.

SUPERPOWER #17: LEADERSHIP SKILLS

Leadership skills are the ability to guide, inspire, and influence others toward achieving a common goal. This superpower involves setting a positive example, providing clear direction, and motivating individuals or teams to perform at their best. It requires effective communication, decision-making, and the ability to assess situations and delegate responsibilities. Mastering leadership skills means understanding how to bring out the strengths of others, manage challenges, and foster an environment where collaboration and growth can thrive.[3]

Captain America's leadership shines not just because of his strength but because of his ability to inspire others to unite for a common cause, even when the odds seem impossible.

As you help the young people in your life develop their leadership skills, you're teaching them to lead with integrity, empathy, and confidence. Encourage them to listen to others, to lead by example, and to be decisive when needed. By fostering the superpower of leadership skills, you're preparing them to take on leadership roles in their communities, schools, and future careers, helping them to become the kind of leaders who inspire and uplift those around them.

Leadership by Example

Leading by example means modeling the behaviors, attitudes, and work ethic you want others to follow. When you lead by example, you demonstrate the standards you expect, showing rather than telling others what is important. This approach is about integrity and consistency—doing what you say and setting a positive precedent for others to emulate. People are more likely to trust and respect a leader who practices what they preach. In your role, focus on showing dedication, being accountable, and treating others with respect to inspire those around you to do the same.[4]

Positive Reinforcement

Positive reinforcement is a strategy used to encourage desired behavior by rewarding it. When you use positive reinforcement, you give praise, recognition, or other rewards immediately after someone does something well. This approach reinforces that behavior, making it more likely to be repeated. In your role, look for opportunities to acknowledge good work and progress, no matter how small, because it motivates others and builds their confidence. Whether it's offering a compliment, giving a high-five, or just saying "well done," positive reinforcement is a powerful tool for building a supportive and motivated environment.[5]

Training Missions for Children

Here are some practical activities children can engage in to cultivate leadership skills.

- **Organize a group project.** Whether it's at school, in a club, or among friends, encourage your children to take the lead in organizing a group project. This could be anything from a small science experiment to a community cleanup effort. Guide them to delegate tasks, set goals, and ensure everyone contributes, teaching them the importance of collaboration and accountability.[6]
- **Lead by example.** Challenge your children to be a role model for their peers. This can be as simple as being kind to others, helping out at home, or demonstrating good sportsmanship in games. Discuss how their actions can positively influence those around them and the importance of consistency in leadership.[7]
- **Take on a mentorship role.** If your children excel in a particular subject or skill, encourage them to help a peer

who might be struggling. This builds confidence and teaches patience and the value of sharing knowledge—a key leadership trait.[8]

- **Volunteer for leadership roles.** Encourage your children to volunteer for leadership positions in extracurricular activities, such as becoming a class representative, team captain, or club leader. These roles provide real-world experience in managing responsibilities, motivating others, and making decisions.[9]

- **Reflect on leadership experiences.** After each leadership experience, take time to reflect with your children. Discuss what went well, what challenges they faced, and what they learned. This reflection helps solidify their understanding of leadership and how to improve in future roles.[10]

By engaging in these activities, your children will begin to understand that leadership is not just about being in charge but also about inspiring others, making thoughtful decisions, and taking responsibility for their actions.

In the 2014 film *Captain America: The Winter Soldier*, during the climactic battle, Captain America (Steve Rogers) leads a critical mission to stop Hydra from using S.H.I.E.L.D.'s helicarriers to carry out mass eliminations. Despite facing overwhelming odds, Steve steps up, delivering an inspiring speech to the S.H.I.E.L.D. agents, urging them to stand up for what's right. He clearly outlines the plan and motivates his team to take action, even at great personal risk. This scene showcases Captain America's leadership by example, as he not only inspires others to follow a moral path but also ensures that everyone understands their role in the mission, fostering a united effort.[11]

Developing leadership skills in your children prepares them to inspire and guide others while making thoughtful decisions. By encouraging them to take initiative, lead by example, and collaborate with peers, you help them build the confidence and responsibility needed to lead effectively. Leadership skills enable your children to influence positive outcomes, motivate others, and navigate group dynamics with integrity. As they develop this superpower, your children will be better equipped to take on leadership roles and contribute meaningfully to their communities and beyond.

ACTION ITEMS

- Before you read further, take a few minutes to consider the information presented in this section.
- Imagine your children decades in the future (after many years of cultivating leadership skills) and how they use this superpower to achieve their goals.
- Note how your children currently employ leadership skills in their daily life. Take pride in the progress they've already achieved in developing this superpower.
- Evaluate the effectiveness of your current practices to help your children cultivate these skills.
- If you decide that your current efforts to help your children cultivate leadership skills need to be improved, consider at least one improvement you can make in the coming weeks, months, or year.
- Develop a plan for implementing that improvement.

Now that we've addressed the superpower of leadership skills, let's move on to emotional intelligence.

SUPERPOWER #18: EMOTIONAL INTELLIGENCE

Emotional intelligence, EQ, is the ability to recognize, understand, and manage your own emotions while also being attuned to the emotions of others. This superpower involves self-awareness, empathy, and emotional regulation, allowing you to navigate social interactions with sensitivity and understanding. It requires the ability to identify emotional cues in yourself and others, respond appropriately to emotional situations, and maintain balance in emotionally charged circumstances. Mastering emotional intelligence means developing strong relationships, managing stress, and adapting to emotional dynamics with awareness and control.[12]

Captain America's emotional intelligence enables him to stay calm in high-pressure situations, read the emotions of his teammates, and offer the empathy and understanding needed to bring them together.

As you guide the young people in your life to develop their emotional intelligence, you're helping them become more self-aware, empathetic, and emotionally resilient. Encourage them to reflect on their feelings, to practice active listening, and to respond to others with compassion and understanding. By fostering the superpower of emotional intelligence, you're equipping them to lead emotionally balanced lives and to build deep, meaningful connections with others.

Training Missions for Children

Here are some activities children can engage in to cultivate emotional intelligence.

- **Emotion identification game.** Start by labeling emotions during daily interactions. For example, when your children are upset, help them identify their feelings by saying, "It looks like you're feeling sad." Encourage them to express how they feel in words, helping them expand their emotional vocabulary.[13]

- **Role-playing scenarios.** Create role-playing situations where your children can practice empathy. For instance, take turns acting out how different characters might feel in a story. Ask questions like, "How do you think they feel?" and "What could you do to help?"[14]
- **Emotion journaling.** Introduce your children to the concept of an emotion journal. Encourage them to write or draw about their feelings each day, focusing on what made them feel a certain way and how they responded. This activity helps them reflect on their emotions and understand their triggers.[15]
- **Mindful breathing.** Teach your children simple mindful breathing exercises to help them manage overwhelming emotions. Practice together by taking deep breaths and focusing on calming thoughts when emotions run high. This will equip them with tools to regulate their feelings in stressful situations.[16]

By consistently engaging your children in these activities, you will help them build the superpower of emotional intelligence, empowering them to understand and manage their emotions effectively while nurturing meaningful connections with others.

In the 2016 film *Captain America: Civil War*, when the Avengers are divided over the Sokovia Accords, Steve Rogers exemplifies emotional intelligence by acknowledging and respecting the differing opinions within the team. While he firmly opposes the Accords, Steve listens to Tony Stark's perspective, understanding the guilt and sense of responsibility driving Tony's stance. Despite the escalating conflict, Steve remains composed, demonstrating empathy for his teammates' emotional states while staying true to his own principles. His ability to manage both his own emotions and those of others in high-pressure situations highlights his emotional intelligence, enabling him to maintain relationships and effectively navigate the complex dynamics of the team.[17]

Fostering emotional intelligence in your children helps them understand and manage their own emotions while empathizing with others. By guiding them to recognize their feelings, communicate effectively, and respond thoughtfully to the emotions of those around them, you equip them to build strong, healthy relationships. Emotional intelligence allows your children to navigate social interactions with compassion and self-awareness. As they develop this superpower, your children will be better prepared to handle emotional challenges, foster positive connections, and contribute to a supportive and understanding environment.

ACTION ITEMS

- Before you read further, take a few minutes to consider the information presented in this section.
- Imagine your children decades in the future (after many years of cultivating emotional intelligence) and how they use this superpower to achieve their goals.
- Note how your children currently employ emotional intelligence in their daily life. Take pride in the progress they've already achieved in developing this superpower.
- Evaluate the effectiveness of your current practices to help your children cultivate these skills.

- If you decide that your current efforts to help your children cultivate emotional intelligence need to be improved, consider at least one improvement you can make in the coming weeks, months, or year.
- Develop a plan for implementing that improvement.

Now that we've addressed the superpower of emotional intelligence, let's move on to teamwork.

SUPERPOWER #19: TEAMWORK

Teamwork is the collaborative effort of a group of individuals working together toward a common goal or objective. It involves effective communication, mutual respect, cooperation, and the ability to leverage the diverse strengths of team members. Successful teamwork requires individuals to set aside personal agendas, trust one another, and contribute their skills to achieve shared success, often resulting in more innovative solutions and better outcomes than could be accomplished alone.[18]

Captain America's ability to rally diverse groups—whether it's his fellow Avengers or a band of soldiers—highlights how teamwork thrives when everyone's unique strengths are valued and directed toward a common goal.

As you help the young people in your life develop their teamwork skills, you're teaching them to value collaboration and to understand the power of working together. Encourage them to listen to others, to share their ideas, and to support their teammates in pursuit of common goals. By fostering the superpower of teamwork, you're equipping them to contribute positively to any group, whether in school, sports, or their future careers, and to understand the true strength that comes from unity and collaboration.

Training Missions for Children

Here are some activities children can engage in to cultivate teamwork.

- **Teamwork projects.** Encourage your children to participate in group projects or activities, such as building a model, organizing a play, or planning a small event. Assign each child a role and encourage them to collaborate, share ideas, and support one another. This activity teaches children how to work as part of a team, communicate effectively, and respect others' contributions.[19]
- **Sports and games.** Involve your children in team sports or cooperative games where they must work with others to win or achieve a goal. These activities teach valuable lessons about collaboration, leadership, and the role each person plays in a team's success.[20]
- **Discuss teamwork in stories.** Read books or watch movies that highlight teamwork. Afterwards, discuss with your children how the characters worked together, what challenges they faced, and how they overcame obstacles by relying on each other's strengths.[21]

By consistently engaging in these activities, your children will develop the superpower of teamwork, enabling them to collaborate effectively, respect diverse perspectives, and contribute meaningfully to any group effort.

In the 2012 film *The Avengers*, during the Battle of New York, Captain America works seamlessly with his fellow Avengers to defend the city against the Chitauri invasion. Demonstrating his ability to quickly assess each team member's strengths, he efficiently coordinates their efforts, assigning roles that maximize the team's effectiveness. For example, he directs Iron Man to contain the perimeter and Hulk to handle the heaviest firepower. This scene highlights Captain America's exceptional teamwork skills, as he leads by example and fosters collaboration, ensuring that the team's combined efforts result in success.[22]

Teaching your children the value of teamwork encourages them to collaborate effectively with others, share responsibilities, and work toward common goals. By helping them understand the importance of communication, cooperation, and mutual respect, you guide them in becoming a valuable team player. Teamwork skills enable your children to contribute positively to group efforts, navigate diverse perspectives, and achieve success through collective action. As they develop this superpower, your children will be better equipped to work harmoniously with others in a variety of settings, fostering a sense of community and shared achievement.

ACTION ITEMS

- Before you read further, take a few minutes to consider the information presented in this section.
- Imagine your children decades in the future (after many years of cultivating teamwork) and how they use this superpower to achieve their goals.
- Note how your children currently employ teamwork in their daily life. Take pride in the progress they've already achieved in developing this superpower.
- Evaluate the effectiveness of your current practices to help your children cultivate these skills.

- If you decide that your current efforts to help your children cultivate teamwork need to be improved, consider at least one improvement you can make in the coming weeks, months, or year.
- Develop a plan for implementing that improvement.

Now that we've addressed the superpower of teamwork, let's move on to responsible citizenship.

SUPERPOWER #20: RESPONSIBLE CITIZENSHIP

Responsible citizenship is the practice of actively contributing to the well-being of one's community and society by upholding ethical standards, respecting laws, and promoting positive social change. It involves being informed about local and global issues, participating in civic duties such as voting, volunteering, and advocating for justice, and demonstrating respect for others. Responsible citizens are accountable for their actions, engage in civic activities, promote the common good, and obey the law.[23]

Captain America's unwavering commitment to justice and protecting the greater good makes him the ultimate role model for responsible citizenship, showing that leadership is about serving others and standing up for what's right.

As you guide the young people in your life to develop their sense of responsible citizenship, you're teaching them the importance of being active and informed participants in society. Encourage them to learn about the issues that affect their community, to think critically about the impact of their actions, and to contribute in ways that align with their values. By fostering the superpower of responsible citizenship, you're preparing them to become conscientious, compassionate individuals who are committed to making a difference in the world.

Training Missions for Children

Here are some activities children can engage in to cultivate responsible citizenship.

- **Community service projects.** Encourage your children to participate in community service projects, such as helping at a local food bank, planting trees, or participating in neighborhood cleanups. These activities foster a sense of responsibility and commitment to the well-being of others. You can create simple activities like mock elections or recycling challenges to make these concepts more engaging and relatable.[24]
- **Cultural awareness.** Expose your children to different cultures and communities through books, films, and events. Discuss the importance of respecting and understanding people from various backgrounds, promoting inclusivity and empathy.[25]
- **Volunteer together.** Find opportunities to volunteer as a family, whether it's at a local charity, an animal shelter, or a community event. This hands-on experience helps your children see the direct impact of their actions on others and the community. An online search for volunteer opportunities in your community may provide helpful ideas.[26]
- **Family discussions on current events.** Engage in regular discussions about current events and social issues. Encourage your children to express their thoughts and consider different perspectives. This helps them develop critical thinking skills and a deeper understanding of the world around them.[27]

By involving your children in these activities, you'll help them build the superpower of responsible citizenship, empowering them to contribute positively to their community and make informed, ethical decisions in their daily lives.

> In the 2011 film *Captain America: The First Avenger*, even before gaining his superpowers, Steve Rogers exemplifies responsible citizenship by persistently attempting to enlist in the military during World War II, despite being repeatedly rejected due to his physical limitations. Motivated by a deep sense of duty, Steve is determined to serve and protect his country, famously declaring, "I don't like bullies—I don't care where they're from." His unwavering desire to fight for justice, even without powers, defines his strong sense of civic responsibility. This situation underscores Steve's belief that leadership isn't about power—it's about standing up for others and contributing to the greater good, a principle that guides him throughout his journey.[28]

Teaching your children the importance of responsible citizenship helps them understand their role in contributing to the well-being of their community and society. By guiding them to be informed, respectful, and engaged members of their community, you foster a sense of duty and empathy. Responsible citizenship empowers your children to take action in ways that benefit others, whether through volunteering, being environmentally conscious, or participating in civic duties. As they develop this superpower, your children will be better prepared to make positive contributions to the world around them, understanding the impact of their actions on a larger scale.

ACTION ITEMS

- Before you read further, take a few minutes to consider the information presented in this section.
- Imagine your children decades in the future (after many years of responsible citizenship) and how they use this superpower to achieve their goals.
- Note how your children currently employ responsible citizenship in their daily life. Take pride in the progress they've already achieved in developing this superpower.
- Evaluate the effectiveness of your current practices to help your children cultivate these skills.
- If you decide that your current efforts to help your children cultivate responsible citizenship need to be improved, consider at least one improvement you can make in the coming weeks, months, or year.
- Develop a plan for implementing that improvement.

Captain America exemplifies the superpowers of leadership, emotional intelligence, teamwork, and responsible citizenship. His leadership is not just about being at the forefront of battles but also about connecting deeply with his teammates, fostering unity and trust through empathy. By respecting each team member's unique strengths and using them toward a shared goal, he shows that teamwork is more than collaboration—it's about valuing differences. His unwavering commitment to justice and service highlights that leadership is about uplifting others and making ethical choices. Captain America's story demonstrates that these traits are interconnected and accessible to anyone willing to embrace them, inspiring us to strive for greatness in ourselves and our communities.[29]

Leadership and teamwork shape how your children contribute to their communities, support others, and take responsibility for their actions. When they develop leadership skills, they learn to guide with integrity and lead by example. When they strengthen emotional intelligence, they become more aware of their own feelings and the needs of those around them. When they practice teamwork, they understand the value of collaboration and shared success. And when they embrace responsible citizenship, they recognize their role in making their world a better place. By nurturing these abilities, you help them grow into individuals who uplift others, work toward common goals, and take an active part in shaping the future.

In the next chapter, we'll explore how embracing habit and routine management, time management, information management, money management, and career management can further empower your children to become real-life superheroes.

6

PRACTICAL LIFE MANAGEMENT

This chapter introduces the core elements of practical life management—where the art of habit and routine, the science of time management, the precision of information management, the strategy of money management, and the foresight of career planning intersect. Mastering these skills lays the foundation for a life defined by growth, fulfillment, and excellence.

Think of Black Widow, a superhero whose success isn't just a result of her combat abilities, but of her exceptional talent for balancing complex aspects of her life with skill and precision—an embodiment of practical life management at its best.[1]

Let's begin with habit and routine management.

SUPERPOWER #21: HABIT AND ROUTINE MANAGEMENT

Habits and routines are often confused because they seem so similar—after all, routines frequently include habits. But understanding the difference between the two is key to managing your day effectively. Let's break them down and see what sets them apart.

- *Habits* are actions or behaviors that are repeated regularly and tend to occur subconsciously. They are developed through repetition over time, becoming automatic responses to certain cues or triggers. Examples include brushing your teeth every morning or checking your phone as soon as you wake up. Once they're ingrained, habits often require minimal thought.[2]
- *Routines* are more deliberate sets of actions performed in a specific sequence to achieve a desired outcome. While they can eventually become habitual, routines usually involve conscious planning and decision-making. An example is a morning routine that includes exercising, showering, and making breakfast. Unlike habits, routines require active effort and are often more structured.[3]

Both habits and routines are essential for effective habit and routine management, helping individuals maintain consistency and structure in their daily lives.

Black Widow's disciplined lifestyle shows the power of maintaining strong habits and routines. Her commitment to daily training ensures she's always ready for any challenge.

Routines

A well-structured routine is like a blueprint for your day, outlining where your time and energy will be directed. Routines are a collection of linked habits and actions organized into a specific sequence to help you achieve a consistent outcome. Think of routines as a way to automate your life so you can focus on more complex goals and ambitions.[4]

Components of a Routine

A well-structured routine is built from key components that work together to create consistency, efficiency, and purpose in daily life.

- **Trigger or cue.** Each routine starts with a trigger—a signal that prompts you to begin the sequence. This could be waking up, arriving at school, or finishing homework.
- **Actions or habits.** These are the behaviors performed in a specific order. For example, a morning routine might include stretching, brushing your teeth, eating breakfast, and reviewing your daily goals.
- **Sequence and timing.** Routines are about the order and duration of actions. Having a consistent structure is crucial, but it should also be flexible enough to adjust when necessary.
- **Purpose or outcome.** Every routine should be designed with a purpose, such as optimizing your morning, enhancing focus before a study session, or unwinding before sleep.

Creating Effective Routines

To build a solid routine, follow this step-by-step process.[5]

1. **Define your purpose.** Identify what you want the routine to accomplish. Is it to improve productivity, maintain focus, or care for your physical health? Write down the goal so you have a clear target.

2. **List the actions.** Break down each action needed to achieve that purpose. Start with the essential habits and add in supportive actions. For example, a study routine could include clearing your desk, reviewing your notes, setting a timer, and taking breaks.

3. **Order and optimize.** Arrange these actions in a logical sequence, grouping similar activities together to maximize efficiency. Consider the best order to maintain momentum and keep things flowing smoothly. For instance, physical activities like stretching or exercise should come before mentally demanding tasks like problem-solving.

4. **Set time blocks.** Assign a realistic amount of time to each action. This helps prevent procrastination and ensures you're not rushing through the routine. For example, if you're creating a morning routine, set aside enough time to complete it without feeling rushed.

5. **Create a trigger.** Choose a consistent trigger that will cue your routine to start. This could be a specific time of day or an event, like getting home from school or hearing your alarm clock ring.

6. **Test and adjust.** Implement the routine for a week and observe how it fits into your life. Are some actions taking longer than expected? Do you feel more focused or stressed? Adjust the sequence, time blocks, or specific actions based on what's working or needs improvement.

7. **Refine and repeat.** Routines should evolve over time. As your priorities change, update your routines to reflect new goals or interests. Regularly refining your routines keeps them effective and aligned with your long-term vision.

By following this process, you can create routines that serve your goals and reduce decision fatigue, helping you stay on track even when life gets busy.

How to Form a New Habit

Forming a new habit can feel like unlocking a superpower within yourself, one that transforms small daily actions into a routine that serves your long-term goals. Here's a process to help you develop any new habit, step by step.[6]

1. **Start with a clear intention.** Decide on a specific habit you want to develop. Instead of saying, "I want to exercise more," say, "I will walk for thirty minutes every day after school." By being clear and specific, you give your brain a simple target to focus on.

2. **Anchor it to an existing routine.** To make this new habit stick, connect it to something you already do daily. For example, if you want to practice mindfulness, tie it to brushing your teeth each morning. You could say to yourself, "After I brush my teeth, I will spend five minutes in mindfulness." Linking your new habit to a routine you already have makes it easier to remember and follow through.

3. **Start small and be consistent.** It's tempting to go big, but lasting habits are built by consistency, not size. If you want to read more, start with just ten minutes daily. The key is making the habit easy enough to do it daily, no matter what. Remember, the goal is to show up consistently—even when you don't feel like it.

4. **Use a trigger and reward system.** Set up a system that reminds you to do the habit (the trigger) and rewards you when you complete it. For example, if your habit is studying for twenty minutes after dinner, the act of finishing dinner is your trigger. Once you've completed your study session, reward yourself with something simple, like listening to your favorite song. The trigger-

reward loop reinforces the habit in your brain, making it easier to repeat.

5. **Track your progress.** Use a journal, a habit-tracking app, or a simple calendar to mark each day you successfully complete your habit. Tracking your progress helps you see how far you've come and motivates you to keep going. There's power in watching a streak build up, and it pushes you to avoid breaking the chain.

6. **Be patient and adjust as needed.** It takes time to build a new habit, so be patient with yourself. If you miss a day, don't be discouraged—just pick up where you left off. If the habit isn't sticking, adjust it. Maybe you need to simplify it or shift the time of day when you do it. Stay flexible and committed, knowing that every small step counts.[7]

By following these steps, you'll transform the act of forming a new habit into a superpower you can use to build the life you want.

How to Break a Bad Habit

Breaking a bad habit can feel like taking back control over your actions, allowing you to direct your energy toward more positive, empowering behaviors. Here's a process that can help you successfully break a bad habit.[8]

1. **Identify the habit and its triggers.** The first step in breaking a bad habit is to recognize it clearly. Be specific about the habit you want to stop, whether it's procrastination, biting your nails, or excessive screen time. Then, take a closer look at what triggers the habit. Do you tend to procrastinate when you're stressed, or reach for your phone out of boredom? Understanding the situations,

emotions, or environments that lead to the habit will help you gain control over it.

2. **Replace the habit with a positive action.** Instead of just focusing on stopping the habit, think about what you can do instead. It's easier to replace a bad habit with a good one than to simply stop altogether. If you want to cut down on mindless snacking, for example, you could replace it with drinking water or going for a short walk when you feel the urge. The key is to swap the negative behavior for something that supports your well-being.

3. **Make it hard to continue the habit.** One of the most effective ways to break a habit is to make it difficult to keep doing it. If your bad habit is spending too much time on social media, try deleting the apps from your phone or setting strict time limits. If it's eating junk food, don't keep it in the house. By making the habit less convenient, you'll reduce the chances of slipping back into it.

4. **Use reminders to stay on track.** You can't rely on willpower alone to break a bad habit. Set up reminders to help you stay on course. These could be notes or alarms that remind you of your goal, or even a friend or family member who can help hold you accountable. For example, if you're trying to stop overspending, leave reminders like "Do I really need this?" on your wallet or phone to pause before making a purchase.

5. **Track your progress and reward yourself.** Tracking your progress helps keep you motivated. Whether it's a journal or an app, record each day you avoid the bad habit. Celebrate your small wins along the way with rewards. For instance, if you manage to go a week without falling into the habit, treat yourself to something that doesn't undermine your progress. Positive reinforcement strengthens your commitment to change.

6. **Be patient and persistent.** Breaking a bad habit takes time and effort, so be patient with yourself. It's normal to have setbacks but don't let them discourage you. If you slip up, acknowledge it, and refocus on your goal the next day. Each day is a new opportunity to make progress—over time, the bad habit will lose its hold on you.[9]

By following these steps, you'll be on your way to breaking the bad habit and replacing it with behaviors that bring you closer to the life you want.

Training Missions for Children

Here are some activities children can engage in to cultivate habit and routine management.

- **Create a daily schedule.** Collaborate with your children to design a balanced daily schedule that includes time for schoolwork, chores, play, and relaxation. Encourage consistency in following the routine and set aside time each week to review and adjust it as needed. This practice reinforces the value of structure and helps them develop strong time management skills.[10]
- **Morning and evening routines.** Establish simple morning and evening routines with your children. For example, they might make their bed in the morning, brush their teeth, and have breakfast. In the evening, they could set out their clothes for the next day, pack their school bag, and read before bed. These routines help your children start and end their day with a sense of order and accomplishment.[11]
- **Habit tracker.** Introduce your children to the concept of a habit tracker. Together, choose a few positive habits they'd

like to develop, such as reading daily, practicing a musical instrument, or tidying up their room. Use a chart or app to track their progress, celebrating milestones along the way to reinforce consistency.[12]

- **Goal setting.** Help your children set small, achievable goals related to their habits and routines. For example, if they want to improve their homework routine, set a goal of completing their assignments by a certain time each day. Break down larger goals into manageable steps, teaching them the value of persistence and discipline.[13]

By engaging in these activities, your children will develop the skills to create a balanced, organized life that supports their long-term goals and well-being.

In the 2019 film *Avengers: Endgame*, Black Widow (Natasha Romanoff) oversees operations at Avengers HQ. She maintains a strict routine of checking in with various heroes across the universe, organizing missions, and ensuring the continuity of their efforts after the catastrophic event where Thanos wiped out half of all life in the universe. This showcases her discipline and habit of consistent leadership. Her regular check-ins with her team demonstrate how she applies routine management to keep things organized and running smoothly despite overwhelming challenges. When Natasha talks with Okoye, Rocket, Captain Marvel, and others during a holographic meeting, she is focused and systematic, ensuring the team stays on track with their individual missions. This reflects how habits and routines help her maintain order amidst chaos.

Helping your children develop strong habits and routines equips them with the tools to manage their time effectively and stay organized. By encouraging consistency and structure in their daily activities, you support them in achieving their goals and maintaining a balanced lifestyle. Habit and routine management enables your children to build discipline, reduce stress, and create a sense of stability in their life. As they cultivate this superpower, your children will be better prepared to navigate responsibilities with confidence and efficiency, laying the groundwork for success in all areas of their life.

ACTION ITEMS

- Before you read further, take a few minutes to consider the information presented in this section.
- Imagine your children decades in the future (after many years of cultivating habit and routine management) and how they use this superpower to achieve their goals.
- Note how your children currently employ habit and routine management in their daily life. Take pride in the progress they've already achieved in developing this superpower.
- Evaluate the effectiveness of your current practices to help your children cultivate these skills.
- If you decide that your current efforts to help your children cultivate habit and routine management need to be improved, consider at least one improvement you can make in the coming weeks, months, or year.
- Develop a plan for implementing that improvement.

Now that we've addressed the superpower of habit and routine management, let's move on to time management.

SUPERPOWER #22: TIME MANAGEMENT

Time management is the strategic life skill of organizing, planning, and controlling how you spend your time to achieve specific goals. It involves setting priorities, creating schedules, and making conscious decisions about how much time to dedicate to various tasks. By mastering this skill, you learn how to balance competing demands, ensuring that your focus remains on what matters most. Time management is not about doing everything but about making deliberate choices that align with your objectives and values. It requires discipline, foresight, and adaptability, allowing you to efficiently navigate short-term and long-term projects.[14]

Black Widow expertly juggles her roles as an Avenger and a spy, evidence of her time-management skills. Her ability to prioritize tasks and act quickly in high-stakes situations shows how you can make the most of your time to stay focused and productive.

Overcoming Procrastination

Procrastination is delaying or postponing tasks, often choosing to do something more enjoyable or less challenging. While it may feel like a temporary escape, procrastination can lead to increased stress, missed opportunities, and a sense of being overwhelmed. By learning how to overcome procrastination, you and your children can build strong time management skills and develop the discipline to take control of responsibilities.[15]

One of the most effective ways to combat procrastination is to adopt a mindset of tackling the most difficult or important tasks first. Mark Twain famously said, "If it's your job to eat a frog, it's best to do it first thing in the morning. And if it's your job to eat two frogs, it's best to eat the biggest one first."[16] This means that if you or your children have a challenging or unpleasant task to complete, it's best to get it done early in the day before distractions and excuses take over.

Encourage your children to identify their "frogs" each day—their biggest, most important tasks—and complete them first. This habit not only builds productivity but also strengthens self-discipline and resilience. When the hardest task is out of the way, the rest of the day feels easier and more manageable.

Another helpful strategy is the **five-minute rule**—if a task feels overwhelming, commit to working on it for just five minutes. More often than not, getting started is the hardest part, and once momentum builds, it's easier to continue.[17]

Time blocking can also help. Encourage your children to set aside specific time slots for homework, chores, or projects. By structuring their time and minimizing distractions, they can develop focus and efficiency.[18]

Procrastination may be tempting, but overcoming it is a powerful ability. By teaching your children to take action, prioritize effectively, and develop a proactive mindset, you are helping them cultivate lifelong skills that will serve them well in school, work, and beyond.

Training Missions for Children

Here are some activities children can engage in to cultivate time management.[19]

- **Prioritization practice.** Teach your children how to prioritize tasks by creating a "to-do list" together. Help them identify which tasks are urgent, which are important, and which can wait. This will help them learn to manage their time by focusing on what truly matters first.[20]

- **Time estimation game.** Turn time management into a fun challenge by asking your children to estimate how long different activities will take, such as homework, chores, or getting ready for bed. Then, time the activities to see how accurate their estimates were. This activity helps them become more aware of how they spend their time and how to plan accordingly.[21]
- **Use a visual timer.** Introduce your children to the concept of using a timer to manage tasks. For instance, set a timer for twenty minutes for reading or ten minutes for tidying up. The visual representation of time passing can help them stay focused and develop a sense of urgency.[22]
- **Weekly planning session.** Sit down with your children at the beginning of each week to plan out their activities. Discuss what needs to be done for school, extracurriculars, and leisure time. This helps them see the bigger picture and understand the importance of balancing various responsibilities.[23]
- **Time management reflection.** At the end of the day or week, encourage your children to reflect on how they spent their time. Ask questions like, "What went well?" and "What could you do differently next time?" This reflection process helps them become more intentional with their time and learn from their experiences.[24]

By consistently engaging in these activities, your children will develop the superpower of time management, empowering them to use their time wisely, stay organized, and achieve their goals with greater efficiency and ease.

Throughout the Marvel Cinematic Universe, Black Widow is known for her quick decision-making and time management, especially under pressure. In *Captain America: The*

Winter Soldier (2014), Black Widow and Captain America (Steve Rogers) infiltrate S.H.I.E.L.D.'s undercover facility. Natasha efficiently divides her time between disabling security, gathering intel, and executing the mission, showing her ability to manage limited time during high-stress scenarios. When Steve and Natasha are on the run, she demonstrates how to prioritize tasks efficiently. Her quick thinking and ability to delegate what needs to be done immediately, while still focusing on long-term goals, is a great example of effective time management.

Teaching your children time management skills helps them prioritize tasks, set goals, and use their time effectively. By guiding them to plan their days, manage deadlines, and balance their responsibilities, you equip them with the tools to accomplish more with less stress. Time management allows your children to take control of their schedule, make intentional choices, and be more productive. As they develop this superpower, your children will be better prepared to meet challenges, stay organized, and make the most of their time in both personal and academic pursuits.

ACTION ITEMS

- Before you read further, take a few minutes to consider the information presented in this section.
- Imagine your children decades in the future (after many years of cultivating time management) and how they use this superpower to achieve their goals.
- Note how your children currently employ time management in their daily life. Take pride in the progress they've already achieved in developing this superpower.
- Evaluate the effectiveness of your current practices to help your children cultivate these skills.

- If you decide that your current efforts to help your children cultivate time management need to be improved, consider at least one improvement you can make in the coming weeks, months, or year.
- Develop a plan for implementing that improvement.

Now that we've addressed the superpower of time management, let's move on to information management.

SUPERPOWER #23: INFORMATION MANAGEMENT

Information management is the strategic life skill of collecting, organizing, storing, and using data or knowledge in an efficient and effective manner. It involves identifying the most relevant and accurate information for a particular task or decision, as well as ensuring that the information is accessible and usable when needed. This superpower includes filtering out unnecessary or irrelevant data, maintaining a system for organizing information, and continually updating your knowledge base to stay current. Information management requires attention to detail, a structured approach, and the ability to discern credible sources from unreliable ones, allowing you to make informed decisions.[25]

As a spy, Black Widow knows the importance of gathering and organizing information. Her success often depends on having the correct data at the right time.

As you guide the young people in your life to develop their information management skills, you're teaching them how to handle information with care and precision. Encourage them to be selective about the sources they trust, to organize their information in a way that makes it easy to retrieve, and to apply what they learn in practical situations. By fostering the superpower of information management, you're equipping them to navigate the complexities of the information age with confidence and competence.

Training Missions for Children

Here are some activities children can engage in to cultivate information management.

- **Organize school materials.** Encourage your children to keep their school materials organized. Help them create a system for their notes, assignments, and resources, such as using folders or digital tools. This will teach them the importance of having easy access to information when they need it.[26]
- **Research projects.** Assign your children a small research project on a topic they are interested in. Guide them in finding reliable sources, taking notes, and organizing the information they gather. This exercise will help them develop skills in sorting through information and discerning what's important.[27]
- **Create a family information center.** Set up a family bulletin board or digital calendar where important dates, reminders, and contact information are posted. Involve your children in maintaining this center, which helps them understand the value of keeping information easily accessible and up-to-date.[28]
- **Teach digital literacy.** Introduce your children to the basics of digital literacy, such as how to safely search for information online, recognize credible sources, and avoid misinformation. Practice these skills together by researching a fun topic and discussing how to verify the accuracy of the information you find.[29]

- **Information categorization game.** Turn information management into a game by asking your children to categorize different types of information. For example, give them a mix of grocery items, school supplies, and household tasks, and ask them to sort these into appropriate categories. This activity reinforces the skill of organizing information logically.[30]

By engaging in these activities, your children will develop the superpower of information management, enabling them to effectively navigate and utilize the vast amount of information they encounter in their daily lives, both in school and beyond.

In the 2021 film *Black Widow*, Natasha Romanoff has to gather and manage a vast amount of sensitive information about the Red Room. She carefully pieces together the puzzle of who controls the Red Room and how to bring it down. She knows how to find, protect, and use information strategically, reflecting excellent information management skills. Natasha's ability to track down old information from Dreykov's daughter and use it to exploit weaknesses in the Red Room shows her mastery of gathering, analyzing, and managing critical information to achieve her goals.

Teaching your children how to manage information helps them navigate the vast amount of data they encounter daily. By guiding them to organize, evaluate, and use information effectively, you prepare them to make informed decisions and solve problems efficiently. Information management skills enable your children to filter through resources, retain important knowledge, and apply what they learn in meaningful ways. As they develop this superpower, your children will be better equipped to handle academic tasks, personal projects, and future challenges with confidence and clarity.

ACTION ITEMS

- Before you read further, take a few minutes to consider the information presented in this section.
- Imagine your children decades in the future (after many years of cultivating information management) and how they use this superpower to achieve their goals.
- Note how your children currently employ information management in their daily life. Take pride in the progress they've already achieved in developing this superpower.
- Evaluate the effectiveness of your current practices to help your children cultivate these skills.
- If you decide that your current efforts to help your children cultivate information management need to be improved, consider at least one improvement you can make in the coming weeks, months, or year.
- Develop a plan for implementing that improvement.

Now that we've addressed the superpower of information management, let's move on to money management.

SUPERPOWER #24: MONEY MANAGEMENT

Money management is the strategic life skill of understanding how to effectively handle your finances—which encompasses earning, saving, budgeting, spending, and investing. It involves making intentional decisions about how to allocate your money to meet both short-term needs and long-term goals. This superpower requires you to track your income and expenses, create a budget that aligns with your priorities, and make responsible choices about saving and investing. By incorporating investments, you not only plan for your future but also seek ways to grow your wealth over time. Money management also includes preparing for unexpected expenses and making informed financial choices that support your overall financial well-being.[31]

Black Widow is resourceful, knowing how to manage limited resources under pressure. Her ability to plan and budget for missions mirrors how you can handle your finances—by saving, budgeting, and making smart investments for the future.

As you help the young people in your life develop their money-management skills, you're teaching them to value money as a tool for achieving their dreams and goals. Encourage them to set financial goals, to budget their income, and to make informed choices about spending and saving. By fostering the superpower of money management, you're equipping them to build a financially secure future and to make wise decisions that will benefit them throughout their lives.

Training Missions for Children

Here are some activities children can engage in to cultivate money management.

- **The allowance system.** Start by giving your children a weekly allowance in exchange for completing age-appropriate chores. This teaches them the value of earning money and the importance of fulfilling responsibilities. Encourage them to divide their allowance into three categories: saving, spending, and giving. This simple practice introduces the concept of budgeting and helps them understand the importance of balancing immediate desires with long-term goals and generosity.[32]

- **Setting savings goals.** Help your children set a savings goal for something they really want, like a toy or a game. Break down the cost into smaller, achievable savings targets. Encourage them to track their progress in a notebook or an app designed for kids. Celebrate milestones along the way to keep them motivated and reinforce the satisfaction that comes with achieving financial goals.[33]
- **The power of comparison shopping.** Take your children shopping, either in-person or online, and show them how to compare prices for the same item at different stores. Discuss the importance of value and quality, not just the price. This activity helps them become more conscious consumers and teaches them that patience and research can lead to better financial decisions.[34]
- **Family budgeting discussions.** Involve your children in family budgeting discussions, appropriate to their age. Explain how you allocate money for necessities, savings, and fun. You might even let them help decide how to spend a portion of the family entertainment budget. This inclusion fosters a sense of responsibility and gives them a realistic understanding of financial planning.[35]
- **Money-management games.** Introduce your children to board games or apps that simulate real-life money-management scenarios. Games like Monopoly, The Game of Life, or educational apps designed to teach financial literacy can make learning about money fun and engaging. These games also encourage strategic thinking and decision-making, which are essential components of effective money management.[36]

By engaging in these activities, your children will begin to understand the value of money, the importance of saving and budgeting, and the satisfaction of making informed financial decisions.

> Though money management is not overtly portrayed, Natasha Romanoff's ability to live off the grid and resourcefully manage her finances can be inferred throughout *Black Widow* (2021). She operates without the support of government resources or S.H.I.E.L.D. funding after being declared a fugitive. Her ability to travel, secure supplies, and maintain her lifestyle speaks to her savvy financial management. Natasha's nomadic life in Black Widow suggests that she has the means to live frugally yet efficiently. She stays off the radar, purchasing essentials without drawing attention to herself, which speaks to practical money management—spending wisely, planning ahead, and managing assets effectively.

Teaching your children money-management skills equips them to handle financial decisions with confidence and responsibility. By guiding them to save, spend wisely, and understand the value of money, you prepare them to navigate the financial aspects of their life effectively. Money management helps your children set financial goals, make informed choices, and develop habits that lead to financial stability. As they develop this superpower, your children will be better prepared to manage their resources, avoid financial pitfalls, and achieve their future goals with a solid understanding of how to use money wisely.

ACTION ITEMS

- Before you read further, take a few minutes to consider the information presented in this section.
- Imagine your children decades in the future (after many years of cultivating money management) and how they use this superpower to achieve their goals.
- Note how your children currently employ money management in their daily life. Take pride in the progress they've already achieved in developing this superpower.
- Evaluate the effectiveness of your current practices to help your children cultivate these skills.
- If you decide that your current efforts to help your children cultivate money management need to be improved, consider at least one improvement you can make in the coming weeks, months, or year.
- Develop a plan for implementing that improvement.

Now that we've addressed the superpower of money management, let's move on to career management.

SUPERPOWER #25: CAREER MANAGEMENT

Career management is the strategic life skill of actively planning and directing your professional journey. It involves setting career goals, developing the skills and qualifications needed to achieve those goals, and making informed decisions about education, job opportunities, and career growth. This superpower requires ongoing self-assessment, adaptability, and a focus on building a strong professional network. Career management also encompasses navigating workplace dynamics, seeking out mentorship, and continually refining your personal brand. It's about taking ownership of your career trajectory and being proactive in shaping your professional future.[37]

Black Widow's career showcases adaptability and strategic growth. From a spy to an Avenger, she's always refining her skills and navigating new challenges. Like her, you can manage your career by setting clear goals, learning new skills, and staying adaptable.

As you help the young people in your life develop their career management skills, you're teaching them to think proactively about their future and to take intentional steps toward building a fulfilling career. Encourage them to explore their interests, seek out learning opportunities, and plan their career path with both short-term and long-term goals in mind. By fostering the superpower of career management, you're equipping them to navigate the complexities of the professional world and to create a career that brings them success, satisfaction, and a sense of purpose.

Training Missions for Children

Here are some activities children can engage in to develop career management skills.

- **Exploring interests and strengths.** Encourage your children to explore a variety of hobbies and activities, from sports to arts to science experiments. Observe which activities they naturally gravitate toward and excel in. Discuss how their interests and strengths might relate to different careers. This helps them begin to identify potential career paths and understand the importance of aligning work with passion and skills.[38]
- **Career research projects.** Choose a career that interests your children and help them research what it involves. They

can look up the education required, daily responsibilities, and potential earnings. You might also arrange for them to interview a family friend or community member who works in that field. This activity not only broadens their understanding of different careers but also teaches them how to seek out information and make informed decisions.[39]

- **Setting long-term goals.** Guide your children in setting long-term goals related to their career interests. For instance, if he or she dreams of becoming a veterinarian, they can set goals like excelling in science classes or volunteering at an animal shelter. Break these goals into smaller, manageable steps, and encourage them to track their progress. This instills the importance of planning and perseverance in achieving career aspirations.[40]

- **Role-playing and job simulation.** Engage your children in role-playing activities where they take on different careers. They could pretend to be a teacher, doctor, chef, or any other profession of interest. You can set up simple scenarios or even create a mini "office" or "workplace" at home. This playful activity not only sparks imagination but also helps them visualize themselves in various careers and understand the roles and responsibilities involved.[41]

- **Developing a personal brand.** Teach your children the basics of creating a personal brand. Discuss the importance of a good reputation, both online and offline. Encourage them to consider how they want to be perceived by others and the values they aspire to be recognized for. You can help them create a simple portfolio showcasing their achievements, talents, and projects. This activity introduces the concept of self-presentation and the significance of building a positive image in their future career.[42]

By engaging in these activities, your children will explore their interests, set goals, and understand the importance of continuous learning and self-improvement, all of which are key to navigating a successful career path.

> Natasha Romanoff's journey in the Marvel Cinematic Universe is an excellent example of career management, from her time as a Russian spy to becoming an Avenger. In *Black Widow* (2021), Natasha confronts her past while managing her present identity as a hero. She makes strategic career decisions, transitioning from a S.H.I.E.L.D. agent to a superhero, and even takes control of her narrative by breaking away from her former controllers. For example, when Natasha decides to face the Red Room in *Black Widow*, she demonstrates her ability to manage her career trajectory, balancing her past and future. By severing ties with toxic influences and taking control of her legacy, she models how to take charge of one's career development and growth.

Helping your children develop career-management skills prepares them to navigate their future with purpose and direction. By guiding them to explore their interests, set career goals, and plan for the steps needed to achieve those goals, you equip them with the tools to build a fulfilling and successful career. Career management skills enable your children to make informed decisions about their education and work opportunities, adapt to changes in the job market, and pursue a path that aligns with their strengths and passions. As they develop this superpower, your children will be better positioned to take charge of their professional journey with confidence and clarity.

ACTION ITEMS

- Before you read further, take a few minutes to consider the information presented in this section.
- Imagine your children decades in the future (after many years of cultivating career management) and how they use this superpower to achieve their goals.
- Note how your children currently employ career management in their daily life. Take pride in the progress they've already achieved in developing this superpower.
- Evaluate the effectiveness of your current practices to help your children cultivate these skills.
- If you decide that your current efforts to help your children cultivate career management need to be improved, consider at least one improvement you can make in the coming weeks, months, or year.
- Develop a plan for implementing that improvement.

Like Black Widow, your children can develop the skills to manage their life with purpose and control. Her success isn't just about physical strength—it's built on discipline, careful planning, and the ability to adapt to any situation. She relies on well-honed habits and routines to stay prepared, manages her time with precision, gathers and processes information efficiently, makes calculated financial decisions, and navigates her career with strategy and foresight. When your children strengthen these same abilities, they set themselves up for a future where they can handle responsibilities, seize opportunities, and move through life with confidence. Practical life management isn't just about getting through the day—it's about shaping a path forward, just as Black Widow does with every mission she undertakes.

Practical life management gives your children the foundation to navigate daily responsibilities and long-term goals with confidence. When they build strong habits and routines, they create structure that supports their growth. When they manage their time well, they make space for learning, work, and personal fulfillment. When they organize and use information effectively, they sharpen their decision-making. When they understand money management, they develop financial independence. And when they explore career management, they prepare for a future that aligns with their strengths and ambitions. By helping them develop these skills, you equip them to handle challenges, seize opportunities, and take charge of their own success.

In the next chapter, we'll explore how embracing numeracy, technology skills, and learning skills can further empower your children to become real-life superheroes.

7

TECHNOLOGY AND LEARNING SKILLS

In today's fast-paced world, mastering the ability to learn is one of the most valuable skills you can develop. Learning isn't just about absorbing information—it's about understanding how to approach new challenges and adapt to a constantly changing environment. This chapter focuses on three key life skills that form the foundation of effective learning: numeracy, technology skills, and learning skills.

We can draw inspiration from Cyborg, a superhero whose essence combines advanced technology and human intellect, reflecting the importance of being technologically savvy and adaptable today.[1]

Given that many technological applications and tools require a fundamental grasp of numerical concepts, our journey begins with numeracy.

SUPERPOWER #26: NUMERACY

Numeracy is the ability to understand and work with numbers, applying mathematical concepts and reasoning to everyday situations. It involves performing calculations, interpreting data, recognizing patterns, and solving quantitative problems. This skill encompasses not only basic arithmetic but also a deeper comprehension of how numbers relate to each other, whether in finance, measurements, or statistics. Numeracy allows individuals to make informed decisions, analyze information, and approach challenges with a logical and methodical mindset.[2]

Cyborg's analytical abilities highlight the importance of numeracy in today's data-driven world. His mastery of complex calculations and pattern recognition allows him to process vast amounts of data in seconds.

As you help the young people in your life develop their numeracy skills, you're teaching them to approach the world with a logical, analytical mindset. Encourage them to practice mental math, to understand the practical applications of numbers, and to use numeracy as a tool for making informed decisions. By fostering the superpower of numeracy, you're equipping them to excel in an analytics-centric era and to make choices that are grounded in clear, accurate understanding.

Training Missions for Children

Here are some activities children can engage in to cultivate numeracy.

- **Number games and puzzles.** Introduce your children to fun and interactive number games and puzzles. Activities like sudoku, math-based board games, or apps designed to improve math skills can make learning numbers enjoyable. These games encourage logical thinking, pattern recognition, and problem-solving, all of which are vital components of numeracy.[3]

- **Real-life math challenges.** Incorporate math into everyday activities. Ask your children to help you measure ingredients while cooking, calculate the total cost while shopping, or count change during a purchase. These practical applications help them see the relevance of math in daily life and reinforce their ability to perform basic calculations with confidence.[4]

- **Story problems.** Create simple math story problems that relate to your children's interests. For example, if they love animals, you could ask, "If there are three birds on a tree and two more join them, how many birds are there now?" This not only makes math fun but also helps them develop their ability to apply math concepts to real-world scenarios.[5]

- **Building with blocks and shapes**. Engage your children in building activities using blocks, LEGO, or other construction toys. Encourage them to count the pieces, estimate the number of blocks needed to complete a structure, or explore geometric shapes. This hands-on experience enhances their understanding of spatial relationships, measurement, and geometry.[6]

- **Math journaling.** Encourage your children to keep a math journal where they can solve problems, draw shapes, and explore math concepts creatively. You can introduce challenges like "How many ways can you make the number ten?" or "Draw and label different types of triangles." This activity fosters a positive attitude toward math and enables children to express their understanding in a personal and meaningful way.[7]

- **Time-telling and calendar activities.** Teach your children
  to tell time[8] and use a calendar.[9] You can make a daily
  routine of checking the time together, planning activities,
  or counting down the days to a special event. These
  activities reinforce the concept of time and help them
  develop skills in reading clocks and managing schedules.

By engaging in these activities, your children will learn to
approach numbers and math with confidence, apply mathematical
thinking to everyday situations, and develop a lifelong appreciation for the value of strong numeracy skills.

In the 2021 film *Zack Snyder's Justice League*, Cyborg (Victor
Stone) exemplifies advanced numeracy skills through his
ability to manipulate global financial systems. One standout
scene demonstrates his mastery when he accesses and
reconfigures complex financial data streams to assist a
struggling woman, depositing a substantial sum of money
into her bank account. This moment highlights his technical prowess and underscores how numeracy extends
beyond mere calculations—it involves interpreting data and
recognizing patterns that can profoundly impact people's
lives.[10]

Teaching your children numeracy skills equips them to navigate
the world of numbers with confidence and understanding. By
guiding them to engage with math in everyday situations, solve
problems, and recognize patterns, you help them build a strong
foundation for academic and practical success. Numeracy enables
your children to make informed decisions, understand financial
concepts, and approach challenges logically. As they develop this
superpower, your children will be better prepared to apply mathematical thinking in various aspects of life, enhancing their ability

to manage tasks, solve problems, and succeed in both personal and academic endeavors.

ACTION ITEMS

- Before you read further, take a few minutes to consider the information presented in this section.
- Imagine your children decades in the future (after many years of cultivating numeracy) and how they use this superpower to achieve their goals.
- Note how your children currently employ numeracy in their daily life. Take pride in the progress they've already achieved in developing this superpower.
- Evaluate the effectiveness of your current practices to help your children cultivate these skills.
- If you decide that your current efforts to help your children cultivate numeracy need to be improved, consider at least one improvement you can make in the coming weeks, months, or year.
- Develop a plan for implementing that improvement.

Now that we've addressed the superpower of numeracy, let's move on to technology skills.

SUPERPOWER #27: TECHNOLOGY SKILLS

Technology skills refer to the ability to effectively use and interact with digital tools, software, and devices. These skills encompass a wide range of competencies, including understanding how to navigate computer systems, use various applications, and work with devices like smartphones, tablets, and computers. Technology skills also involve knowing how to troubleshoot common issues, manage online platforms, and stay updated with emerging technologies. They include both basic functions, such as using word processors and communication tools, and more advanced tasks like coding, data analysis, and working with specialized software or hardware. Mastery of these skills allows individuals to adapt to a rapidly changing digital landscape, ensuring they can operate efficiently and confidently in various environments.[11]

Cyborg's integration of technology into his very being illustrates the power of tech skills in modern life. His ability to seamlessly interact with digital systems, solve technical problems, and adapt to new software and hardware demonstrates how crucial it is to stay current with evolving technology. By mastering tech skills, you, too, can navigate the digital landscape like Cyborg, using technology as a tool to enhance your capabilities and solve challenges creatively.

As you guide the young people in your life to develop their technology skills, you're equipping them to thrive in a digital age. Encourage them to embrace technology as a tool for learning, creativity, and innovation. Teach them to be responsible digital citizens, to continuously update their skills, and to use technology to enhance their lives and the lives of others. By fostering the superpower of technology skills, you're preparing them to navigate and shape the future with confidence and competence.

Training Missions for Children

Here are some activities children can engage in to cultivate technology skills.

- **Basic coding projects.** Introduce your children to the basics of coding through age-appropriate apps and websites like Scratch, Code.org, or Tynker. These platforms offer fun, interactive lessons where your children can create simple games, animations, and stories. Coding helps develop problem-solving skills, logical thinking, and creativity—core components of technology proficiency.[12]

- **Digital research and information literacy.** Teach your children how to safely search for information online. You can guide them through the process of using search engines, evaluating the credibility of sources, and summarizing their findings. This activity not only enhances their research skills but also instills a sense of responsibility in using the internet wisely.[13]

- **Using educational software.** Encourage your children to explore educational software that enhances learning in various subjects, such as math, science, or language arts. These tools often incorporate interactive elements that make learning engaging and reinforce their understanding of key concepts through technology.[14]

- **Responsible social media use.** If your children are old enough, teach them how to use social media responsibly. Discuss the importance of privacy, the impact of their digital footprint, and how to communicate respectfully online. This activity fosters digital citizenship and ensures they develop healthy habits in navigating the social aspects of technology.[15]

- **Building digital projects.** Encourage your children to create digital projects, such as a simple website,[16] a digital scrapbook,[17] or a presentation on a topic of interest. These projects can be done using accessible tools like Google Slides, Canva, or basic website builders. This activity allows them to practice their design, organization, and presentation skills while gaining confidence in using different types of technology.[18]

- **Exploring robotics and engineering kits.** Introduce your children to robotics and engineering kits, like LEGO Mindstorms, Ozobot, or other STEM-focused toys. These kits allow them to build and program robots,[19] exploring the intersection of technology and engineering. This hands-on experience is both educational and exciting, nurturing their interest in how technology can be applied in real-world scenarios.[20]
- **Creating and editing digital media.** Teach your children how to take photos, record videos, and edit them using basic software like iMovie or Photoshop Express. You can work together on a family project, such as making a video diary or creating a photo collage. This activity not only builds their technical skills but also encourages creativity and storytelling.[21]

By engaging in these activities, your children will learn to approach digital tools with confidence, understand the importance of responsible online behavior, and develop the technical acumen needed to thrive in an increasingly digital world.

In the 2021 film *Zack Snyder's Justice League*, Cyborg (Victor Stone) showcases his exceptional technology skills throughout the story. His cybernetic enhancements grant him the ability to interface seamlessly with any digital system. Notably, he hacks into alien technology, decoding the workings of the Mother Boxes and devising a plan to prevent their unification. His effortless command of both terrestrial and extraterrestrial systems underscores his mastery of digital and physical technology. This illustrates that true technological expertise goes beyond merely using tools—it's about innovating new applications and solutions in critical, high-stakes situations.[22]

Teaching your children technology skills prepares them to navigate an increasingly digital world with confidence and competence. By guiding them to understand and use various digital tools, solve problems with technology, and stay informed about the latest advancements, you equip them to leverage technology in their learning and everyday life. Technology skills enable your children to access information, communicate effectively, and innovate in ways that are essential for personal and professional growth. As they develop this superpower, your children will be better prepared to adapt to the demands of the modern world and use technology to achieve their goals and enhance their experiences.

ACTION ITEMS

- Before you read further, take a few minutes to consider the information presented in this section.
- Imagine your children decades in the future (after many years of cultivating technology skills) and how they use this superpower to achieve their goals.
- Note how your children currently employ technology skills in their daily life. Take pride in the progress they've already achieved in developing this superpower.
- Evaluate the effectiveness of your current practices to help your children cultivate these skills.
- If you decide that your current efforts to help your children cultivate technology skills need to be improved, consider at least one improvement you can make in the coming weeks, months, or year.
- Develop a plan for implementing that improvement.

Now that we've addressed the superpower of technology skills, let's move on to learning skills.

SUPERPOWER #28: LEARNING SKILLS

Learning skills refer to the ability to effectively acquire, process, and retain new information, allowing individuals to adapt to changing environments and challenges. These skills include techniques for understanding and remembering material, such as note-taking, summarizing, and applying knowledge in different contexts. Learning skills also encompass critical aspects like curiosity, self-discipline, and staying focused and organized when tackling new subjects. They involve developing strategies for problem-solving, understanding complex concepts, and applying different learning methods, such as visual, auditory, or kinesthetic techniques, to suit various needs.[23]

Cyborg's constant upgrades and adaptability exemplify the superpower of learning skills. His ability to continually evolve by integrating new technologies reflects the importance of lifelong learning. Like Cyborg, you can stay ahead of the curve by developing effective learning strategies, constantly improving your abilities, and staying curious about the world around you.

As you guide the young people in your life to develop their learning skills, you're teaching them the importance of being lifelong learners. Encourage them to explore their interests, to experiment with different learning strategies, and to view mistakes as valuable learning experiences. By fostering the superpower of learning skills, you're equipping them to navigate an ever-evolving world with curiosity, adaptability, and a passion for growth.

Training Missions for Children

Here are some activities children can engage in to cultivate learning skills.

- **Reading for pleasure.** Encourage your children to read regularly by providing a variety of books that match their interests. Create a cozy reading nook and set aside time each day for reading. Discuss the stories together, ask questions about the plot and characters, and encourage them to share their thoughts. This activity not only improves literacy but also fosters a love for learning and curiosity about the world.[24]
- **Active note-taking.** Teach your children to take effective notes while studying or listening to a lesson. Show them different methods, such as summarizing key points, creating mind maps, or using color coding to organize information. Active note-taking helps them engage more deeply with the material and enhances their ability to retain and recall information.[25]
- **Exploring different learning styles.** Introduce your children to various learning styles—visual, auditory, kinesthetic, and reading/writing. Encourage them to experiment with different methods, such as watching educational videos, listening to audiobooks, or participating in hands-on activities. By discovering what works best for them, they'll develop a personalized approach to learning that maximizes their strengths.[26]
- **Using educational games and apps.** Incorporate educational games and apps into your children's learning routine. Many of these tools are designed to make learning fun and interactive, reinforcing concepts through play. Whether it's math, language arts, or science, these games can make difficult subjects more accessible and enjoyable.[27]
- **Reflective learning.** After completing a project or learning a new concept, encourage your children to reflect on the process. Ask them questions like, "What was the

most challenging part?" or "What did you enjoy the most?" This reflective practice helps them understand their learning journey, identify areas for improvement, and appreciate their progress.[28]

By engaging in these activities, your children will learn how to approach new information with confidence, set and achieve goals, and enjoy the process of learning as a lifelong pursuit.

In the 2021 film *Zack Snyder's Justice League*, Cyborg (Victor Stone) is in a constant state of learning and adaptation as he navigates his newly acquired abilities, including the power to interface with technology on a global scale. As he evolves into his new form, Cyborg embarks on a journey of self-discovery, learning to control his advanced technological interfaces and powers while deepening his understanding of his connection to the world's digital networks. His learning process exemplifies self-directed, adaptive, and resilient skills. Rather than merely accepting his new capabilities, Cyborg actively learns to harness them in increasingly creative ways, ultimately contributing to the team's success.[29]

Helping your children develop strong learning skills prepares them to approach new information with curiosity and confidence. By encouraging them to explore different methods of learning, set goals, and reflect on their progress, you equip them with the tools to continuously grow and adapt. Learning skills enable your children to acquire knowledge effectively, think critically, and apply what they learn in meaningful ways. As they develop this superpower, your children will be better prepared to face challenges, embrace new opportunities, and pursue lifelong learning with enthusiasm and determination.

ACTION ITEMS

- Before you read further, take a few minutes to consider the information presented in this section.
- Imagine your children decades in the future (after many years of cultivating learning skills) and how they use this superpower to achieve their goals.
- Note how your children currently employ learning skills in their daily life. Take pride in the progress they've already achieved in developing this superpower.
- Evaluate the effectiveness of your current practices to help your children cultivate these skills.
- If you decide that your current efforts to help your children cultivate learning skills need to be improved, consider at least one improvement you can make in the coming weeks, months, or year.
- Develop a plan for implementing that improvement.

Think again of Cyborg, who seamlessly blends cutting-edge technology with human intuition and intellect to overcome challenges. Numeracy, technology skills, and learning skills prepare your children to meet the demands of the modern world where they hope to excel. Cyborg's ability to adapt his technological components for various scenarios mirrors the flexibility and innovative thinking required of tomorrow's leaders. Embracing these superpowers enables you to not only navigate but also shape the future, leveraging technology as a tool for unprecedented achievements. As we close this chapter, remember that, like Cyborg, your children can harness technology to extend your capabilities, solve complex problems, and transform obstacles into opportunities.[30]

Technology and learning skills shape how your children adapt, grow, and engage with the world around them. When they develop numeracy, they strengthen their ability to think logically and make informed decisions. When they build technology skills, they learn to navigate digital tools with confidence and responsibility. When they embrace learning as a lifelong process, they open themselves to new ideas, challenges, and possibilities. These abilities give them the tools to solve problems, stay curious, and keep evolving in an ever-changing world. By encouraging these skills, you help them approach the future with knowledge, adaptability, and a mindset for growth.

In the conclusion of this book, we'll bring everything together to help you plan your next steps.

SHARE THE MISSION!

We're on a mission to nurture a generation of real-life superheroes, and that means we're going to need more parents on board! Take a moment now to help me reach them by leaving a short review.

Simply by sharing your honest opinion of this book and a little about your own experience, you'll show new readers where they can find the guidance they need to teach their children the skills they need to thrive in the world.

MAKE A LASTING IMPRESSION!

Thank you so much for your support. Here's to a new generation of superheroes!

Scan the QR code below to leave your review on Amazon.

[QR code]

CONCLUSION

THE HERO'S JOURNEY: A FINAL WORD

This journey has been about equipping you with the tools and strategies to help your children grow into mindful, responsible, and well-rounded individuals. Together, we've navigated life's challenges and explored the superpowers needed to overcome them. From mastering emotions and building meaningful relationships to thriving in the digital age and beyond, you now hold a powerful toolkit designed to guide your children through life's trials and help them flourish.

The path of a hero is not defined by the absence of adversity but by the courage to face it head-on. The skills and insights shared in these pages are your children's steadfast allies, illuminating their way during moments of uncertainty. But the real magic lies within your children—their choices, their willingness to embrace challenges, and their unwavering perseverance.

Growth is an ongoing adventure. Each day brings new opportunities for learning and self-improvement. In a rapidly changing world, your children will adapt and thrive with the superpowers they've cultivated, becoming resilient and resourceful as they forge their unique path.

Next Steps: Turning Intentions into Action

This book is packed with actionable advice, more than can be implemented all at once. Remember the wisdom of Desmond Tutu: "How do you eat an elephant? One bite at a time." Start small, focusing on areas that resonate most with your children.

Celebrate Progress

Begin by acknowledging your children's achievements. Every section of this book highlights action steps not only for growth but also for celebrating what your children already do well. These milestones are the foundation of their superpowers. Recognize the contributions of teachers, coaches, and mentors who've played pivotal roles in your children's development. Like Luke Skywalker unknowingly honing his skills on Tatooine by shooting womp rats, your children have been building superpowers all along.

You're Already on the Path

Your children's daily routine—schoolwork, hobbies, family interactions—provides fertile ground for superpower growth. Encourage them to embrace their education and activities with renewed enthusiasm. From tackling homework to participating in extracurriculars, each moment is an opportunity to strengthen their powers. With this mindset, any child can transform into a real-life superhero.

Harvesting Low-Hanging Fruit

Small changes can lead to big results. Encouraging deep-breathing exercises during stressful moments, adding a glass of water to your children's morning routine, or teaching them to "eat the frog" when faced with procrastination may seem minor, but these simple habits add up over time. By helping your children embrace these easy wins, you set the stage for lasting growth—one small step at a time.

Building a Habit of Habits

Superpowers are forged through consistent habits. Help your children cultivate good routines and replace unproductive ones. Each habit they build strengthens their portfolio of life skills. As one behavior becomes ingrained, they can move on to the next, continuously growing closer to their superhero potential.

Goals: The Blueprint for Success

Short-term action steps can guide your children's immediate growth. Create a manageable timeline for these goals, ensuring they remain achievable and enjoyable. Encourage your children to view each challenge as an exciting step on their journey.

For long-term growth, revisit the section on strategic thinking and encourage your children to imagine their future, setting goals that align with their aspirations. By aligning their daily actions with long-term objectives, your children will chart a clear course toward their dreams.

A New Chapter Begins

As this book concludes, your children's adventure is just beginning. Life will present trials and triumphs, but with their superpowers in hand, they'll face each challenge with confidence and grace. Remember, your children are the hero of their own story. Each obstacle is an opportunity to rise, to learn, and to shine.

Encourage your children to keep exploring, growing, and embracing the endless possibilities ahead. The world is vast, filled with mysteries and challenges waiting to be conquered. With the foundation they've built, there are no limits to what they can achieve.

Be the Change

Your journey doesn't end here. By joining forces with other parents committed to raising empowered, emotionally intelligent problem-solvers, you can create meaningful change in your community. Together, you can inspire a generation of real-life superheroes.

To spread this mission, consider leaving a review of this book on Amazon. Your recommendation can help other parents discover the tools they need to guide their children toward a bright and empowered future.

Thank you for allowing me to be part of your journey. This is not just an ending—it's a new beginning. As you turn the page on this book, your children turn the page on their future. May it be filled with courage, wisdom, and the power to change the world.

ENDNOTES

INTRODUCTION

1. Goldstein, "Addressing the Five Greatest Challenges Facing Our Children Today," Dr. Sam Goldstein.
2. The Right Questions, "The 10 Top Life Skills and How to Develop Them."

1. HOLISTIC WELL-BEING

1. Martin, "Holistic Approaches to Well-Being and Health," Creative Healthcare Management.
2. Celebz Post, "Lessons From Batman."
3. Mayo Clinic, "Stress Management."
4. Beresin, "Stress in Teenagers," MassGeneralBrigham.
5. Cleveland Clinic, "Cortisol."
6. ReachOut, "Stress in Teenagers."
7. Coping Skills for Kids, "Deep Breathing Exercises for Kids."
8. Kidsville Pediatrics, "10 Amazing Benefits of Journaling for Kids.
9. Mayo Clinic, "Exercise and Stress: Get Moving to Manage Stress."
10. Harden, "Art Activities for Kids: Using Creativity to Express Emotions," Huckleberry.
11. Quick, "Happy Place Visualization for Kids," Calm Ahoy Kids.
12. Estroff, "The Age-by-Age Guide to Teaching Kids Time Management," Scholastic.
13. Klein, "Create a Safe Place for Your Kids to Share Feelings," Bridges 2 Understanding.
14. Wikipedia, "The Dark Knight Rises."
15. Newsom, "The Connection Between Diet, Exercise, and Sleep," Sleep Foundation.
16. Pearson, "How Omega-3 Fish Oil Affects Your Brain and Mental Health," Healthline.
17. National Cancer Institute, "Antioxidants and Cancer Prevention."
18. Harvard Health Publishing, "Foods Linked to Better Brain Power."
19. Harvard Health Publishing, "Eating to Boost Energy."
20. McIntosh, "What is Serotonin, and What Does It Do?" MedicalNewsToday.
21. Harvard Health Publishing, "How to Boost Your Immune System."
22. Tinsley, "26 Foods to Eat to Gain Muscle," Healthline.
23. Mayo Clinic, "Bone Health: Tips to Keep Your Bones Healthy."
24. Neuhouser, "The Importance of Healthy Dietary Patterns in Chronic Disease Prevention," National Library of Medicine.

25. Mayo Clinic, "Dietary Fat."
26. Mayo Clinic, "Dietary Fat."
27. McIntosh, "15 Benefits of Drinking Water," *MedicalNewsToday*.
28. Johns Hopkins Medicine, "Healthy Eating During Adolescence."
29. Massachusetts General Hospital, "Have Healthy Snacks in Your Diet."
30. Mayo Clinic, "Dietary Fiber: Essential for a Healthy Diet."
31. American Heart Association, "How to Reduce Sodium in Your Diet."
32. John Muir Health, "Nutrition for Teens: Help your teenager develop a healthier relationship with food."
33. Canada's Food Guide, "Healthy Cooking Methods."
34. Gager, "Finding the Hidden Sugar in the Foods You Eat."
35. Johns Hopkins Medicine, "Healthy Eating During Adolescence."
36. Cleveland Clinic, "A Beginner's Guide to Healthy Meal Prep."
37. Prep Dish, "Simple Kids Cooking Activities for Different Stages."
38. The Nest School, "Healthy Food Rainbow Challenge."
39. Run Wild My Child, "Starting an Outdoor Herb Garden with Your Kids."
40. Teachers Pay Teachers, "Supermarket Scavenger Hunt."
41. Action for Healthy Kids, "How to Read Nutrition Facts Labels."
42. Prep Dish, "Easy, Healthy Recipes for Kids to Make (Breakfasts, Snacks & Lunches!).
43. Action for Healthy Kids, "Mindful Eating."
44. Gomez-Penilla, "The Influence of Exercise on Cognitive Abilities," National Library of Medicine.
45. Cox, "Role of Physical Activity for Weight Loss and Weight Maintenance," National Library of Medicine.
46. MedicinePlus, "Benefits of Exercise," National Library of Medicine.
47. MedicinePlus, "Benefits of Exercise," National Library of Medicine.
48. Hinge Health, "12 Bodyweight Exercises PTs Want You to Try."
49. Wikipedia, "High-Intensity Interval Training."
50. Centers for Disease Control and Prevention, "Youth Physical Activity Guidelines."
51. Healthi, "How to Make Physical Activity an Enjoyable Part of Your Lifestyle."
52. Mayo Clinic, "Walking: Trim Your Waistline, Improve Your Health."
53. Commonwealth Pediatrics, "The Benefits of Play: How Playtime Nurtures Child Development."
54. Burke, "5 Tips for Planning the Perfect Outdoor Activity for Everyone," Heat Holders.
55. WebMD, "Benefits of Extracurricular Activities for Kids."
56. Lancia, "Yoga in Education: 7 Poses and Activities for Your Classroom," Positive Psychology.
57. The Learning Center, "Movement and Learning," University of North Carolina at Chapel Hill.
58. MacPherson, "How to Use a Fitness Journal for Goal Tracking." Verywell Fit.
59. Bryan, "Why Do We Need Sleep?" Sleep Foundation.
60. Vandekerckhove and Wang, "Emotion, Emotion Regulation, and Sleep: An Intimate Relationship," National Library of Medicine.

61. Lewis, "How Memory Replay in Sleep Boosts Creative Problem-Solving," National Library of Medicine.

62. Suni, "Mastering Sleep Hygiene: Your Path to Quality Sleep," Sleep Foundation.

63. Pacheco, "Bedtime Routines for Children," Sleep Foundation.

64. National Sleep Foundation, "How to Make a Sleep-Friendly Bedroom."

65. Hale, "Youth Media Screen Habits and Sleep: Sleep-Friendly Screen Behavior Recommendations for Clinicians, Educators, and Parents," National Library of Medicine.

66. Suni, "Sleep Diary," Sleep Foundation.

67. Newsom, "Relaxation Exercises to Help Fall Asleep," Sleep Foundation.

68. Stibich, "10 Benefits of Sleep," Verywell Health.

69. Rocky Mountain Sleeping Baby, "The Role of Nutrition in Your Child's Sleep: Foods That Help or Hinder Rest."

70. The Life and Times of Ben Weinberg, "Anatomy of a Scene—The Training," Medium.

71. Perry, "Get to Know Yourself Through the Act of Self-Reflection," BetterUp.

72. Garey, "The Power of Mindfulness," Child Mind Institute.

73. Perry, "Get to Know Yourself Through the Act of Self-Reflection," BetterUp.

74. Everyday Speech, "Fostering Self-Awareness: Journal Prompts for Elementary Students."

75. Housman Institute, "Reflective Practice in Early Childhood Education."

76. Housman Institute, "Reflective Practice in Early Childhood Education."

77. Croteau, "22 Art Therapy Activities to Help Kids Identify and Manage Their Emotions," We Are Teachers.

78. Morin, "How to Teach Children Gratitude: It's More Than Just Saying Thank You," Verywell Mind.

79. DiYES International School, "The Importance of Goal Setting: Helping Kids Plan and Achieve," LinkedIn.

80. Friday, "Why Storytelling in the Classroom Matters," Edutopia.

81. Fandom, "Rachel Dawes," Batman.

82. Physiopedia, "An Introduction to Mindfulness."

83. Action for Healthy Kids, "Mindful Breathing Exercises."

84. Beck, "Sensory Nature Walk for the Family," The OT Toolbox.

85. Action for Healthy Kids, "Mindful Eating."

86. Zaffarano, "Body Scan Meditation Techniques for Kids," Metro Parent.

87. Ackerman, "25 Fun Mindfulness Activities for Children and Teens (+Tips!)," Positive Psychology.

88. Batts, "Men Are Still Good: An Analysis of Batman in 'Batman v Superman,'" CinemaDebate.

2. CORE PERSONAL DEVELOPMENT

1. Thompson, "Week Five—Spider-Man Learning 'With Great Power Comes Great Responsibility,'" Anchor Counseling Centers.

2. Life and Progress, "Taking Responsibility and Ownership."

3. MYDOH, "10 Printable Chore Charts for Kids with Chore Checklist."

4. Naik, "Examples of Goals for Children (In the Short & Long Term)," GoHenry, Acorns Early.

5. Miller, "Helping Kids Make Decisions," Child Mind Institute.

6. Strong4Life, "Learning from Mistakes: Consequences for Kids," Children's Healthcare of Atlanta.

7. Gunn, "How to Teach Your Child to Be Responsible for Their Things," The Simplicity Habit.

8. DoSomething, "73 Community Service Project Ideas."

9. Trammell, "Family Meetings—An Important Strategy for Creating Good Stewards." Bessemer Trust.

10. Fandom, "Peter Parker."

11. Waco Moms, "A Step-By-Step Guide to Vision Boards for Kids."

12. Children's Wellness Center, "Teaching Kids SMART Goals."

13. Minted, "Celebrate in Style: 31 Creative Ideas for Unforgettable Kid's Birthday Parties."

14. Carrillo, "Strategic Thinking in Children and Adolescents Is Determined by Underlying Network Abilities, " Vox EU, Center for Economic Policy Research.

15. Kidsville Pediatrics, "10 Amazing Benefits of Journaling for Kids."

16. The Kid's Point, "Mind Mapping for Kids: A Creative Tool for Learning."

17. IMDB, "Spider-Man: Homecoming Plot."

18. American Psychological Association, "Resilience Guide for Parents and Teachers."

19. Mostarle, "How Puzzles Help Improve Children's Problem-Solving Skills."

20. Ackerman, "27 Resilience Activities for Children and Adults (+PDF)," Positive Psychology.

21. Clark, "Marion's Story: My Resilience," RecoveryStories.

22. Boland, "How Gratitude Supports Your Child's Emotional Growth," St. Louis Children's Hospital.

23. Ackerman, "25 Fun Mindfulness Activities for Children and Teens (+PDF!)," Positive Psychology.

24. Kong Academy, "Goal Setting for Kids & New Year's Resolutions."

25. Willis, "Guiding Students to Harness Mistakes for Learning," Edutopia.

26. Barry, "'Spider-Man: Far From Home' and Seeing Beyond the Illusions," The Jesuit Post.

27. Wooll, "What is Creative Thinking and How Can I Improve?" BetterUp.

28. Montgomery Child Care Association, "Exploring Different Art Mediums: Painting, Sculpting, and Crafting for Kids."

29. Carepoint Academy, "7 Benefits of Storytelling for Kids."

30. Worley, "Building Projects for Kids," Real Life at Home.

31. Jan Peterson Child Development Center, "Exploring Imaginative Play: Nurturing Creativity in Children."

32. Curiosity Encouraged, "Easy Nature Crafts Your Kids Will Love."

33. Our Family Code, "Tallest Tower STEM Challenge with Only Two Materials."

34. Wikipedia, "Spider-Man: No Way Home."

3. ANALYTICAL AND DECISION-MAKING SKILLS

1. Marvel Cinematic Universe, "Iron Man." Fandom.
2. Wikipedia, "Iron Man."
3. Indeed, "What Are Analytical Skills? Definition, Examples and Tips."
4. Kennedy, "45 Fun and Clever Brain Teasers for Kids with Answers!" Prodigy.
5. Sala, "67 Easy Science Experiments for Kids to Do at Home," Mommy Poppins.
6. Wikipedia, "List of Abstract Strategy Games."
7. Learning at the Primary Pond, "How to Teach Students to Compare and Contrast."
8. Bram, "How to Involve Early Elementary Students in Data Collection," Edutopia.
9. Schwab, "29 Interesting Debate Topics for Kids of All Ages," ClickView.
10. Lemonade Day, "9 Engaging Problem Solving Activities for Kids to Build Critical Skills."
11. IMDB, "Iron Man: Plot."
12. Coursera, "What Are Critical Thinking Skills and Why Are They Important?"
13. Smart, "40 Problem-Solving Techniques and Processes," SessionLab.
14. Lee, "75 Interesting Debate Topics for Kids of All Ages & Grade," SplashLearn.
15. RedClay and Frieden, "Discussion Questions for Use with Any Film That Is a Work of Fiction," TeachWithMovies.
16. Billingsley, "How to Teach Logic: The Best Logic Games for Kids," Dad Suggests.
17. Miss Decarbo, "Compare and Contrast Activity Fun!"
18. Elias, "The Importance of Asking Questions to Promote Higher-Order Competencies." Edutopia.
19. Coiro, "Teaching Adolescents How to Evaluate the Quality of Online Information," Edutopia.
20. Wikipedia, "Iron Man 2."
21. BrightChamps, "Engage and Educate Your Kids with Fun Puzzles for Kids."
22. Frugal Fun for Boys and Girls, "Do a LEGO Bridge Building Challenge!"
23. Twinkl, "Mystery Activities for Kids."
24. Beachboard, "5 Techniques to Promote Divergent Thinking," Edutopia.
25. Lemonade Day! "9 Engaging Problem Solving Activities for Kids to Build Critical Skills."
26. Meredeth, "57 STEM Activities for Kids of All Ages and Interests," We Are Teachers.
27. Science Is Elementary, "Incorporating Problem-Solving into Daily Routines."
28. Never Felt Better, "Review: Iron Man 3."
29. Herrity, "Decision-Making Skills," Indeed.
30. Han, "7 Ways to Improve Your Ethical Decision-Making," Harvard Business School Online.
31. Cooks-Campbell, "Use a Pros and Cons List to Feel Good About Your Decisions," BetterUp.

32. ThinkOrBlue.com, "An Easy Trick to Help Your Child Choose Their Own Clothes."
33. Elke & Curt, "17 Decision-Making Skills for Kids Under 12 That Build Confidence & Independence," Kong Academy.
34. Everyday Speech, "Teaching Decision-Making: Engaging Scenarios for Elementary Students."
35. Everyday Speech, "How to Foster Group Decision-Making Skills in Elementary Students."
36. TeachKloud, "Ethics in Early Years Education."
37. Walker, "Journal Writing as a Teaching Technique to Promote Reflection." National Library of Medicine.
38. Wikipedia, "Avengers: Endgame."

4. COMMUNICATION AND INTERPERSONAL SKILLS

1. Coursera, "What Is Effective Communications? Skills for Work, School, and Life."
2. Friday, "Encouraging Students to Be Storytellers," Edutopia.
3. Your Therapy Source, "Active Listening Games."
4. Morin, "8 Social Situations to Role-Play with Your Middle Schooler," Understood.
5. Stallings, "Promoting Literacy and SEL Through Letter Writing," Edutopia.
6. Aguilar, "10 Ways to Cultivate a Love of Reading in Students," Edutopia.
7. Raising Children Network (Australia), "Nonverbal Communication: Body Language and Tone of Voice."
8. Go Au Pair, "Constructive Criticism for Kids: How to Help Kids Grow."
9. Mikula, "Wonder Woman: Female Strength and the Power of Love," The Bi-College News.
10. Coursera, "What Are Interpersonal Skills?"
11. Manson, "3 Core Components of a Healthy Relationship."
12. Reid, "Empathy," HelpGuide.
13. Marriage In A Box, "Trust and Respect Are the Key to a Healthy Relationship."
14. Poorkavoos, "Eight Behaviors That Build Trust," Roffey Park Institute.
15. Vallejo, "25 Best Empathy Activities for Kids," Mental Health Center Kids.
16. Calm, "How to Teach Kids Good Manners (And Why They Matter)."
17. Bessick, "Compliment Circles: Creating a Kind & Respectful Classroom." The Interactive Teacher.
18. Everyday Speech, "Step-by-Step: Teaching Reflective Listening to Elementary Students."
19. Martines, "Wonder Woman 2017," OpenOregon.
20. The Big Red Group, "Mastering the Art of Negotiation for Teens!"
21. Everyday Speech, "Teaching Compromise and Negotiating Skills to Kindergarten Students."
22. There's Just One Mommy, "Using Pretend Play to Teach Money Skills."

23. Fetsch and Jacobson, "10 Tips for Successful Family Meetings," Colorado State University Extension.

24. FasterCapital, "Child Skills and Negotiation: Negotiation Games for Children: Fun Ways to Teach Valuable Skills."

25. Waters, "How to Teach the Difference Between Wants and Needs: 11 Ideas to Shake Things Up," Erin Waters Education.

26. Twainausten, "Why (& How) to Get Your Homeschool Kids to Journal," Capturing the Charmed Life.

27. Orcena, "Parent's Guide to Helping Teens Through Sibling Relational Problems," Evolve.

28. Mikula, "Wonder Woman: Female Strength and the Power of Love," The Bi-College News.

29. Modern Recovery, "Conflict Resolution."

30. FasterCapital, "Child Skills and Communication: Conflict Resolution for Kids: Teaching Problem-Solving Skills."

31. Gaines, "How to Help Kids Express Big Feelings," Inspired Motherhood.

32. Mediators Beyond Borders International, "Circle Process."

33. LakeCreek Montessori, "Six Steps to Problem Solving."

34. Ibekwe, "20 Conflict Resolution Activities for Kids: Building Harmony Through Play." OsitaIbekwe.com.

35. Lang, "Simple Mediation Methods Can Help Children Resolve Disputes," Mediate.com.

36. Morris, "How to Introduce Journaling to Young Children," Edutopia.

37. Wyatt, "Wonder Woman 2017 Movie Review," Medium.

5. LEADERSHIP AND TEAMWORK

1. Wallace, "10 Leadership Secrets from Captain America," Selling Power.

2. Adler, "Why Captain America Is the Leadership Role Model You Didn't Know You Needed," LinkedIn.

3. Pandey, "What Is Leadership?" Emeritus India.

4. Martins, "How to Lead by Example, According to One Asana Leader," Asana, Inc.

5. Van De Hey, "The Power of Positive Reinforcement," LinkedIn.

6. Pencils to Pigtails, "Easy Science Projects for Preschool and Kindergarten Teachers."

7. Whole Child Counseling, "Activities for Teaching Kids Good Sportsmanship, Teamwork, and Cooperation Skills."

8. Phillips-Jones, "Skills for Successful Mentoring: Competencies of Outstanding Mentors and Mentees."

9. Whalen, "6 Volunteer Projects to Grow and Show Leadership Skills," National Society of High School Scholars (NSHSS).

10. Plaxton, "Reflection: Leadership Lessons Learned as a Child," LinkedIn.

11. IMDB, "Captain America: The Winter Soldier."

12. Cherry, "5 Key Emotional Intelligence Skills," Verywell Mind.

13. Toward Wellbeing, "Emotion Naming Games for Children."
14. Everyday Speech, "Act It Out: A Role-Playing Game to Teach Empathy in the Classroom."
15. ReadTheTale.com, "Introducing Emotional Intelligence: Teaching Kids to Recognize and Express Their Feelings."
16. Fit Sanford Health, "Breathing Techniques to Inspire Mindfulness in Kids."
17. Wikipedia, "Captain America: Civil War."
18. Perry, "What Will Make or Break Your Next Role? Find Out Why Teamwork Matters," BetterUp.
19. Mission Grit, "Teamwork for Kids: Learning the Value in School, Sports and Beyond."
20. Vallejo, "20 Best Cooperative Games for Kids to Foster Teamwork and Collaboration."
21. Moffatt, "Encouraging Greater Collaboration: Top 10 Inspirational Stories of Teamwork Success."
22. IMDB, "The Avengers."
23. Prakash, "Responsible Citizenship: An Essential Element for a Better Society," SarvaYog.
24. DoSomething, "73 Community Service Project Ideas."
25. Tirrell-Corbin, "How to Teach Children about Cultural Awareness and Diversity," PBS Kids/For Parents.
26. DoSomething, "73 Community Service Project Ideas."
27. Nemours Kids Health, "How to Talk to Your Child About the News."
28. IMDB, "Captain America: The First Avenger."
29. Wallace, "10 Leadership Secrets from Captain America," Selling Power.

6. PRACTICAL LIFE MANAGEMENT

1. Marvel Unlimited, "Natasha Romanova: Black Widow."
2. Daoire, "Habit vs. Routine," Shimmer.
3. Arlinghaus, "The Importance of Creating Habits and Routines," National Library of Medicine.
4. Meier, "Habits, Routines, and Rituals," Getting Results.
5. McRae, "How to Start a New Routine and Stick to It," NorthShore, Endeavor Health.
6. Gardner, "Making Health Habitual: The Psychology of 'Habit Formation' and General Practice," National Library of Medicine.
7. Calm, "How Long Does It Take to Create a Habit (And How to Do It)?"
8. American Heart Association, "How to Break Bad Habits and Change Behaviors."
9. Cleveland Clinic, "How to Break Bad Habits."
10. Fernandez, "How to Implement a Simple Daily Schedule for Kids." Organic's Best.
11. Foy, "Practice Super Morning and Bedtime Routines," PBS Kids For Parents.
12. Schulze, "Habit Tracking for Kids: Does It Work?" Joon.

13. Cullins, "4 Steps for Helping Your Child Set Effective Goals," Big Life Journal.
14. Coursera, "What Is Time Management? 6 Strategies to Better Manage Your Time."
15. Cherry, "What Is Procrastination? Why We Keep Putting Things Off, Despite the Consequences," Verywell Mind.
16. BrainyQuote, "Mark Twain Quotes."
17. Cognitive Behavioral Therapy, "End Procrastination with the 5-Minute Rule."
18. Ritchie, "How to Teach Time Management Skills to Kids and Teens," Calendar.
19. Estroff, "The Age-by-Age Guide to Teaching Kids Time Management," Scholastic.
20. Talbert, "How to Prioritize Tasks in 4 Steps (And Get Work Done)," Asana.
21. Henderson, "Fun Time Management Games to Play with Kids," FamilyDaily.
22. Learning Here & There, "How a Timer Can Help Your Kids."
23. Hands On As We Grow, "Learn Sample Weekly Activity Plan."
24. Kumon, "How to Help Your Kids with Time Management Skills."
25. Information School University of Washington, "What Is Information Management?" UW iSchool.
26. Get Organized HQ, "How to Organize Kid's School Papers & Memorabilia."
27. Studentreasures Publishing, "17 Fun Research Projects for Elementary Students."
28. Busy Budgeter, "How to Create a Family Command Center That Will Keep Your Whole Family Organized."
29. University of San Diego Professional and Continuing Education, "A Teacher's Guide to Digital Literary & Digital Literacy Skills in the Classroom."
30. Alice Ferguson Foundation, "Game: Classified Information."
31. Capital One, "7 Money Management Tips to Help You Improve Your Finances."
32. Lake, "Allowances and Kids: How to Build Wealth Habits Early," Investopedia.
33. Focus Federal Credit Union, "Teaching Kids to Set Savings Goals."
34. Payton, "The Importance and Benefits of Comparison Shopping," ShipNetwork.
35. Garza, "How to Teach Kids Budgeting: A Simple Guide for Parents," PrimeWay Federal Credit Union.
36. Fitzsimons Credit Union, "13 Financial Literacy Games for Children and Adults (Gamification Resources)."
37. Ellis, "Career Management: A Detailed Overview," The Knowledge Academy.
38. Connections Academy, "9 Steps for Extracurricular Activities to Help Your Child Find New Hobbies."
39. GoHenry, "Career Exploration for Kids: Help Your Child Choose a Career Path."
40. Cullins, "4 Steps for Helping Your Child Set Effective Goals," Big Life Journal.
41. Northern Illinois University Center for Innovative Teaching and Learning, "Role Playing."
42. Jones, "Teaching Your Child About Personal Branding, " Personal Branding Blog.

7. TECHNOLOGY AND LEARNING SKILLS

1. DC Extended Universe Wiki, "Cyborg."
2. EduBirdie, "Mathematics and Numeracy in Everyday Life," RadioPlus Experts, LTD.
3. Guido, "27 Exciting Math Games for Kids to Skyrocket New Math Skills in the Classroom," Prodigy.
4. Leonard. "11 Real World Math Activities That Engage Students." Edutopia.
5. Peanut Butter Fish Lessons, "14 Types of Math Story Problems."
6. Koralek, "Ten Things Children Can Learn from Block Play." National Association for the Education of Young Children (NAEYC).
7. McAnelly, "How Math Journals Help Students Process Their Learning," Edutopia.
8. We Are Teachers, "33 Fun Time-Telling Games and Activities."
9. Spivey, "Using Calendar Activities to Extend Classroom Learning," Handy-Handouts.
10. Russell, "How Cyborg Became the Heart of Zach Snyder's Justice League," CBR.
11. Coursera, "Technology Skills: What They Are and How to Improve Them."
12. Tynker, "Coding for Kids and Teens Made Easy."
13. WebWise, "Digital Literacy Skills: Finding Information."
14. Juraschka, "Educational Software for Elementary Students: 9 Expert Picks," Prodigy.
15. Cook Center for Human Connection, "10 Ways to Teach Children How to Use Social Media Responsibly."
16. Websults, "How to Teach Website Design to Kids."
17. Gaccione, "5 Easy Steps for Creating Digital Scrapbooks," Teq.
18. Tan, "Breaking Stereotypes: 5 Creative Digital Projects You Can Do with Your Kids."
19. MakerKids, "Robotics for Kids: A Complete Guide for Parents."
20. Home Science Tools, "Engineering Kits."
21. EditMentor, "A Guide to Video Editing by Kids: Tips and Techniques."
22. CBR, "How Cyborg Became the Heart of Zach Snyder's Justice League."
23. Gandi, "Learning Theories," National Library of Medicine.
24. National Library of New Zealand, "Reading for Pleasure: A Door to Success."
25. Staake, "11 Helpful Note-Taking Strategies Your Students Should Know."
26. AbilityPath, "Children's Learning Styles."
27. SkillPrepare, "5 Ways You Can Use Educational Games to Help Your Child Learn."
28. Shea, "Teaching Young Students How to Reflect on Their Learning," Edutopia.
29. CBR, "How Cyborg Became the Heart of Zach Snyder's Justice League."
30. DC Extended Universe, Fandom, "Cyborg."

BIBLIOGRAPHY

"Superheroes Quotes." BrainyQuote. Accessed April 10, 2025. https://www.brainyquote.com/topics/superheroes-quotes.

AbilityPath. "Children's Learning Styles." Accessed December 8, 2024. https://abilitypath.org/ap-resources/childrens-learning-styles/.

Ackerman, Courtney E. "25 Fun Mindfulness Activities for Children and Teens (+PDF!)." Positive Psychology. February 3, 2017. https://positivepsychology.com/mindfulness-for-children-kids-activities/.

Ackerman, Courtney E. "27 Resilience Activities for Children and Adults (+PDF)." Positive Psychology. June 13, 2027. https://positivepsychology.com/resilience-activities-worksheets/.

Action for Healthy Kids. "How to Read Nutrition Facts Labels." Accessed December 30, 2024. https://www.actionforhealthykids.org/activity/how-to-read-nutrition-facts-labels

Action for Healthy Kids. "Mindful Breathing Exercises." Accessed December 27, 2024. https://www.actionforhealthykids.org/activity/mindful-breathing-exercises/.

Action for Healthy Kids. "Mindful Eating." Accessed December 27, 2024. https://www.actionforhealthykids.org/activity/mindful-eating/.

Action for Healthy Kids. "Journaling and Reflective Writing." Accessed December 14, 2024. https://www.actionforhealthykids.org/activity/journaling-and-reflective-writing/.

Adler, Cindy Rella. "Why Captain America Is the Leadership Role Model You Didn't Know You Needed." LinkedIn. January 31, 2019. https://www.linkedin.com/pulse/why-captain-america-leadership-role-model-you-didnt-know-cindy-adler/.

Agboga, Victor. "10 Tips on Note-Taking in Lectures." London School of Economics and Political Science. Accessed June 14, 2024. https://info.lse.ac.uk/current-students/Assets/Articles/10-Tips-on-note-taking-during-lectures.

Aguilar, Elena. "10 Ways to Cultivate a Love of Reading in Students." Edutopia. February 13, 2013. https://www.edutopia.org/blog/cultivating-love-reading-students-elena-aguilar.

Alice Ferguson Foundation. "Game: Classified Information." Accessed December 11, 2024. https://www.fergusonfoundation.org/resources/game-classified-information/.

American Psychological Association. "Resilience Guide for Parents and Teachers." Accessed December 19, 2024. https://www.apa.org/topics/resilience/guide-parents-teachers.

An Adventurous Education. "How to Plan a Project with Your Child." Accessed December 25, 2024. https://www.anadventurouseducation.com/2020/03/28/how-to-plan-a-project-with-your-child/.

Batts, Alex. "Men Are Still Good—An Analysis of Batman in 'Batman v Superman,'" CinemaDebate. March 21, 2019. https://cinemadebate.com/2019/03/21/men-are-still-good-an-analysis-of-batman-in-batman-v-superman/.

Beachboard, Cathleen. "5 Techniques to Promote Divergent Thinking." Edutopia. April 12, 2023. https://www.edutopia.org/article/divergent-thinking-fosters-creativity/.

Beck, Colleen. "Sensory Nature Walk for the Family." The OT Toolbox. March 3, 2021. https://www.theottoolbox.com/sensory-nature-walk-for-the-family/.

Bessick, Paige. "Compliment Circles: Creating a Kind & Respectful Classroom." The Interactive Teacher. Accessed December 15, 2024. https://paigebessick.com/compliment-circles-creating-kind/.

Big Red Education. "Mastering the Art of Negotiation for Teens!" July 23, 2022 https://bigrededucation.com/mastering-the-art-of-negotiation-for-teens/.

Billingsley, Ryan. "How to Teach Logic: The Best Logic Games for Kids." Dad Suggests. Accessed February 9, 2025. https://www.dadsuggests.com/home/the-best-logic-games-for-kids.

Boland, Kelly, PhD. "How Gratitude Supports Your Child's Emotional Growth." St. Louis Children's Hospital. October 30, 2024. https://www.stlouischildrens.org/health-resources/pulse/gratitude-children-emotional-growth

BrainyQuote. "Mark Twain Quotes." Accessed February 12, 2025. https://www.brainyquote.com/quotes/mark_twain_414009.

Bram, Michelle Hart. "How to Involve Early Elementary Students in Data Collection." Edutopia. October 20, 2023. https://www.edutopia.org/article/data-collection-elementary-students/.

Bricks 4 Kidz. "Helping Your Child Explore Their Own Interests." August 12, 2020. https://www.bricks4kidz.com/blog/helping-your-child-explore-their-own-interests/.

BrightChamps. "Engage and Educate Your Kids with Fun Puzzles for Kids." Accessed December 18, 2024. https://brightchamps.com/blog/puzzles-for-kids/.

Bryan, Lucy. "Why Do We Need Sleep?" Sleep Foundation. Updated April 5, 2024. https://www.sleepfoundation.org/how-sleep-works/why-do-we-need-sleep

Burke, Jacqui. "5 Tips for Planning the Perfect Outdoor Activity for Everyone." Heat Holders. March 1, 2024. https://www.heatholders.com/blogs/wow/5-

tips-for-planning-the-perfect-outdoor-activity-for everyone?srsltid=Afm-BOoqbooCpEk7okLOQG4U_cGWyNnYvgnosH-lmXDWZk9wx3hWIHWg5.

Busy Budgeter. "How to Create a Family Command Center That Will Keep Your Whole Family Organized." Accessed December 11, 2024. https://www.busybud geter.com/create-a-family-command-center/.

Calm. "How to Teach Kids Good Manners (And Why They Matter)." Accessed December 15, 2024. https://www.calm.com/blog/good-manners.

Capital One. "7 Money Management Tips to Help You Improve Your Finances." September 19, 2024. https://www.capitalone.com/learn-grow/money-manage ment/money-management-tips/.

Carepoint Academy. "7 Benefits of Storytelling for Kids." February 18, 2022. https://www.carepointeacademy.com/blog/posts/benefits-of-storytelling-for-kids.

Carrillo, Juan D. and Isabelle Brocas. "Strategic Thinking in Children and Adolescents Is Determined by Underlying Network Abilities." Vox EU, Center for Economic Policy Research. October 5, 2017. https://cepr.org/voxeu/columns/strategic-thinking-children-and-adolescents-determined-underlying-network-abilities.

CBR. "How Cyborg Became the Heart of Zach Snyder's Justice League." Accessed December 9, 2024. https://www.cbr.com/zack-snyders-justice-league-cyborg-heart-dcu/.

Cherry, Kendra. "5 Key Emotional Intelligence Skills." Verywell Mind. Updated December 31, 2023. https://www.verywellmind.com/components-of-emotional-intelligence-2795438.

Cherry, Kendra. "What Is Procrastination? Why We Keep Putting Things Off, Despite the Consequences." Verywell Mind. Updated July 7, 2024. https://www.verywellmind.com/the-psychology-of-procrastination-2795944.

Children's Wellness Center. "Teaching Kids SMART Goals." August 24, 2024. https://www.childrenswellnesscenter.com/post/teaching-kids-smart-goals.

Clark, David. "Marion's Story: My Resilience." RecoveryStories. September 17, 2013. https://www.recoverystories.info/marions-story-my-resilience/.

Clever Tykes. "How to Develop Ambition in Children." January 23, 2023. https://clevertykes.com/how-to-develop-ambition-in-children/.

Cognitive Behavioral Therapy. "End Procrastination with the 5-Minute Rule." October 5, 2023. https://cogbtherapy.com/cbt-blog/end-procrastination-5-minute-rule.

Coiro, Julie. "Teaching Adolescents How to Evaluate the Quality of Online Information." Edutopia. Updated August 29, 2017. https://www.edutopia.org/blog/evaluating-quality-of-online-info-julie-coiro.

Commonwealth Pediatrics. "The Benefits of Play: How Playtime Nurtures Child

Development." September 1, 2024. https://commonwealthpeds.com/development-and-play

Connections Academy. "9 Steps for Extracurricular Activities to Help Your Child Find New Hobbies." June 16, 2021. https://www.connectionsacademy.com/support/resources/article/9-steps-for-extracurricular-activities-to-help-your-child-find-new-hobbies/.

Cook Center for Human Connection. "10 Ways to Teach Children How to Use Social Media Responsibly." Accessed December 8, 2024. https://cookcenter.org/10-ways-to-teach-children-how-to-use-social-media-responsibly/.

Cooks-Campbell, Allaya. "Use a Pros and Cons List to Feel Good About Your Decisions." BetterUp. July 11, 2023. https://www.betterup.com/blog/pros-and-cons-list.

Coping Skills for Kids. "Deep Breathing Exercises for Kids." Accessed December 30, 2024. https://copingskillsforkids.com/deep-breathing-exercises-for-kids.

Coursera. "11 Good Study Habits to Develop." Updated December 1, 2023. https://www.coursera.org/articles/study-habits.

Coursera. "How Does AI Disrupt Industries?" Updated July 24, 2024. https://www.coursera.org/articles/ai-disrupt-industry.

Coursera. "Technology Skills: What They Are and How to Improve Them." Updated November 24, 2024. https://www.coursera.org/articles/technology-skills.

Coursera. "What Are Critical Thinking Skills and Why Are They Important?" October 30, 2024. https://www.coursera.org/articles/critical-thinking-skills.

Coursera. "What Are Interpersonal Skills? And How to Strengthen Them." Updated January 31, 2024. https://www.coursera.org/articles/interpersonal-skills.

Coursera. "What Is Effective Communications? Skills for Work, School, and Life." November 14, 2024. https://www.coursera.org/articles/communication-effectiveness?isNewUser=true.

Coursera. "What Is Time Management? 6 Strategies to Better Manage Your Time." Updated October 18, 2024. https://www.coursera.org/articles/time-management.

Croteau, Jeanne. "22 Art Therapy Activities to Help Kids Identify and Manage Their Emotions." We Are Teachers. May 16, 2024. https://www.weareteachers.com/art-therapy-activities/.

Cullins, Ashley. "4 Steps for Helping Your Child Set Effective Goals." Big Life Journal. December 26, 2023. https://biglifejournal.com/blogs/blog/goal-setting-for-kids?srsltid=AfmBOopBuQnCKBRyli2oWsYcpO3D9FGhshnxzRZDmBqVOi1A_V6Wh08P.

Curiosity Encouraged. "Easy Nature Crafts Your Kids Will Love." Accessed December 19, 2024. https://curiosityencouraged.com/easy-nature-crafts/.

DC Extended Universe Wiki, "Cyborg." Accessed December 10, 2024. https://dcex tendeduniverse.fandom.com/wiki/Cyborg.

Derhally, Lena Aburdene. "How (and Why) to Create Emotional Safety for Our Kids." Lifetime Montessori School. Accessed December 30, 2024. https://life timemontessorischool.com/how-and-why-create-emotional-safety-our-kids.

Digital Hill Multimedia, Inc. "Importance of Digital Skills in Today's Workspace." Accessed December 9, 2024. https://www.digitalhill.com/blog/importance-of-digital-skills-in-todays-workplace/.

DiYES International School. "The Importance of Goal Setting: Helping Kids Plan and Achieve." LinkedIn. June 11.2024. https://www.linkedin.com/pulse/impor tance-goal-setting-helping-kids-6lexc/.

DoSomething.Org. "73 Community Service Project Ideas." March 15, 2022. https:// dosomething.org/article/community-service-project-ideas.

EditMentor. "A Guide to Video Editing by Kids: Tips and Techniques." January 22, 2024. https://editmentor.com/blog/a-guide-to-video-editing-for-kids-tips-and-techniques/.

EduBirdie. "Mathematics and Numeracy in Everyday Life." RadioPlus Experts, LTD. https://www.google.com/search?q=EduBirdie%2C+%E2%80%9CMathe matics+and+Numeracy+in+Everyday+Life%2C%E2%80%9D+RadioPlus+Experts%2C+LTD.&rlz=1C1CHWL_en US1059US1059&oq=EduBirdie%2C+%E2%80%9CMathemat ics+and+Numeracy+in+Everyday+Life%2C%E2%80%9D+RadioPlus+Experts%2C+LTD.&gs_lcrp=EgZjaHJvbWUyBggAEEUY OTIHCAEQIRiPAjIHCAIQIRiPAjIHCAMQIRiPAtIBCTIzODNqMGoxNag CALACAA&sourceid=chrome&ie=UTF-8.

Elias, Maurice J. "The Importance of Asking Questions to Promote Higher-Order Competencies." Edutopia. July 8, 2014. https://www.edutopia.org/blog/impor tance-asking-questions-promote-higher-order-competencies-maurice-elias.

Elke & Curt. "17 Decision-Making Skills for Kids Under 12 That Build Confidence & Independence." Kong Academy. August 9, 2024. https://www.kongacademy. org/17-decision-making-skills-for-kids-under-12-that-build-confidence-inde pendence/.

Ellis, Sophia. "Career Management: A Detailed Overview." The Knowledge Academy. November 18, 2024. https://www.theknowledgeacademy.com/blog/ career-management/.

Estroff, Sharon Duke. "The Age-by-Age Guide to Teaching Kids Time Management." Scholastic. Accessed December 30, 2024. https://www.scholastic. com/parents/family-life/parent-child/teach-kids-to-manage-time.html.

Everyday Speech. "Act It Out: A Role-Playing Game to Teach Empathy in the Classroom." Accessed December 12, 2024. https://everydayspeech.com/blog-posts/no-prep-social-skills-sel-activity/act-it-out-a-role-playing-game-to-teach-empathy-in-the-classroom

Everyday Speech. "Developing Critical Thinking: Problem Solving Scenarios for Elementary Students." Accessed December 18, 2024. https://everydayspeech.com/sel-implementation/developing-critical-thinking-problem-solving-scenarios-for-elementary-students/.

Everyday Speech. "Fostering Self-Awareness: Journal Prompts for Elementary Students." Accessed December 27, 2024. https://everydayspeech.com/sel-implementation/fostering-self-awareness-journal-prompts-for-elementary-students/.

Everyday Speech. "How to Foster Group Decision-Making Skills in Elementary Students." Accessed December 16, 2024. https://everydayspeech.com/sel-implementation/how-to-foster-group-decision-making-skills-in-elementary-students/.

Everyday Speech. "Step-by-Step: Teaching Reflective Listening to Elementary Students." Accessed December 15, 2024. https://everydayspeech.com/sel-implementation/step-by-step-teaching-reflective-listening-to-elementary-students/.

Everyday Speech. "Teaching Compromise and Negotiating Skills to Kindergarten Students." Accessed December 14, 2024. https://everydayspeech.com/blog-posts/no-prep-social-skills-sel-activity/teaching-compromise-and-negotiation-skills-to-kindergarten-students/.

Everyday Speech. "Teaching Decision-Making: Engaging Scenarios for Elementary Students." Accessed December 16, 2024. https://everydayspeech.com/sel-implementation/teaching-decision-making-engaging-scenarios-for-elementary-students/.

Facing History & Ourselves. "Strategies for Parents & Teens: Current Events." FHAO: Parent Current Event Resources. Accessed February 18, 2025. https://www.facinghistory.org/sites/default/files/2023-08/FHAO_Parent_Current_Event_Resources.vFinal.pdf

Fandom. "Rachel Dawes." Batman. Accessed December 27, 2024. https://batman.fandom.com/wiki/Rachel_Dawes.

FasterCapital. "Ambition: Aiming Forward: Fueled by Ambition and Determination." Updated June 3, 2024. https://fastercapital.com/content/Ambition--Aiming-Forward--Fueled-by-Ambition-and-Determination.html

FasterCapital. "Child Skills and Communication: Conflict Resolution for Kids: Teaching Problem-Solving Skills." Updated June 21, 2024. https://fastercapital.com/content/Child-Skills-and-Communication--Conflict-Resolution-for-Kids--Teaching-Problem-Solving-Skills.html.

FasterCapital. "Child Skills and Negotiation: Negotiation Games for Children: Fun

Ways to Teach Valuable Skills." Updated June 25, 2024. https://fastercapital. com/content/Child-Skills-and-Negotiation--Negotiation-Games-for-Children--Fun-Ways-to-Teach-Valuable-Skills.html.

Fernandez, Augustina. "How to Implement a Simple Daily Schedule for Kids." Organic's Best. August 15, 2023. https://organicsbestshop.com/blogs/organics bestclub/how-to-implement-a-simple-daily-schedule-for-kids.

Fetsch, R.J. and B. Jacobson. "10 Tips for Successful Family Meetings." Colorado State University Extension. Accessed December 14, 2024. https://extension. colostate.edu/topic-areas/family-home-consumer/10-tips-for-successful-family-meetings/.

Fit Sanford Health. "Breathing Techniques to Inspire Mindfulness in Kids." Accessed December 12, 2024. https://fit.sanfordhealth.org/blog/breathing-tech niques-to-inspire-mindfulness-article.

Fitzsimons Credit Union. "13 Financial Literacy Games for Children and Adults (Gamification Resources)." Accessed December 11, 2024. https://www.fitzsi monscu.com/financial-literacy-games-for-children-and-adults/.

Foy, Chelsea. "Practice Super Morning and Bedtime Routines." PBS Kids For Parents. July 21, 2021. https://www.pbs.org/parents/crafts-and-experiments/ practice-super-morning-and-bedtime-routines.

Friday, Matthew James. "Encouraging Students to Be Storytellers." Edutopia. December 2, 2022. https://www.edutopia.org/article/encouraging-students-to-be-storytellers/.

Friday, Matthew James. "Why Storytelling in the Classroom Matters." Edutopia. July 11, 2014. https://www.edutopia.org/blog/storytelling-in-the-classroom-matters-matthew-friday.

Focus Federal Credit Union. "Teaching Kids to Set Savings Goals." August 11, 2023. https://focusok.com/teach-kids-to-set-savings-goals/.

Foreman, Beth. "Journaling Techniques to Help You Start a Journaling Practice." Accessed December 25, 2024. https://bethforeman.com/journaling-tech niques/.

Frugal Fun for Boys and Girls. "Do a LEGO Bridge Building Challenge!" July 31, 2018. https://frugalfun4boys.com/lego-bridge-building-challenge/.

FutureLearn. "What Is Growth Mindset and How Can You Develop One?" April 25, 2022. https://www.futurelearn.com/info/blog/general/develop-growth-mindset.

Gaccione, Caylie. "5 Easy Steps for Creating Digital Scrapbooks." Teq. April 1, 2022. https://www.teq.com/creating-digital-scrapbooks/.

Gaines, Lauren. "How to Help Kids Express Big Feelings." Inspired Motherhood. August 16, 2021. https://inspired-motherhood.com/improve-communication-using-i-statements/.

Gajula, Shravanaveena. "How to Create a Screen Time Schedule That Actually Works." Wellness Hub. Updated October 26, 2024. https://www.mywell nesshub.in/blog/how-to-create-a-screen-time-schedule-that-actually-works/.

Gandi, Mustafa H., and Pinaki Makherji. "Learning Theories." National Library of Medicine. National Center for Biotechnology Information. NIH. Updated July 17, 2023. https://www.ncbi.nlm.nih.gov/books/NBK562189/.

Garey, Juliann. "The Power of Mindfulness," Child Mind Institute. Accessed December 27, 2024. https://childmind.org/article/the-power-of-mindfulness/.

Garza, Laurie Masera. "How to Teach Kids Budgeting: A Simple Guide for Parents." PrimeWay Federal Credit Union. Accessed December 11, 2024. https://www.primewayfcu.com/blog/teach-kids-budgeting-skills.

Get Organized HQ. "How to Organize Kid's School Papers & Memorabilia." Accessed December 11, 2024. https://getorganizedhq.com/how-to-organize-kids-school-papers-memoribilia/.

Go Au Pair. "Constructive Criticism for Kids: How to Help Kids Grow." October 10, 2024. https://www.goaupair.com/childcare-advice/constructive-criticism-for-kids/.

GoHenry, Inc. "Budgeting for Kids: Fun Ways to Teach Budgeting to Kids." February 22, 2023. https://www.gohenry.com/us/blog/financial-education/budgeting-for-kids-fun-ways-to-teach-budgeting-to-kids.

GoHenry. "Career Exploration for Kids: Help Your Child Choose a Career Path." October 12, 2023. https://www.gohenry.com/uk/blog/family/career-explo ration-for-kids.

Goldstein, Sam. "Addressing the Five Greatest Challenges Facing Our Children Today." Dr. Sam Goldstein. Accessed February 18, 2025. https://samgoldstein. com/resources/articles/general/2024/addressing-the-five-greatest-challenges-facing-our-children-today.aspx.

Grover, Sean. "7 Challenges Kids Face That Have Nothing to Do with Parenting." Psychology Today. May 17, 2021. https://www.psychologytoday.com/us/blog/when-kids-call-the-shots/202105/7-challenges-kids-face-that-have-nothing-to-do-with-parenting.

Guido, Marcus. "27 Exciting Math Games for Kids to Skyrocket New Math Skills in the Classroom." Prodigy. May 27, 2024. https://www.prodigygame.com/main-en/blog/classroom-math-games-for-kids/.

Gunn, Wendy. "How to Teach Your Child to Be Responsible for Their Things." The Simplicity Habit. Accessed December 26, 2024. https://www.thesimplicityhabit. com/how-to-teach-your-child-to-be-responsible-for-their-things/.

Hale, Lauren, et al. "Youth Media Screen Habits and Sleep: Sleep-Friendly Screen Behavior Recommendations for Clinicians, Educators, and Parents." National

Library of Medicine. April 27, 2018. https://pmc.ncbi.nlm.nih.gov/arti
cles/PMC5839336

Hands On As We Grow. "Learn Sample Weekly Activity Plan." Accessed December
12, 2024. https://handsonaswegrow.com/samples-weekly-activities-planner/
learn-week/.

Harden, Liz. "Art Activities for Kids: Using Creativity to Express Emotions."
Huckleberry. Updated September 17, 2024. https://huckleberrycare.com/blog/
art-activities-for-kids-using-creativity-to-express-emotions.

Henderson, Ross. "Fun Time Management Games to Play with Kids." FamilyDaily.
May 21, 2023. https://www.familydaily.app/blog/time-management-games-
for-kids.

Herrity, Jennifer. "Decision-Making Skills," Indeed. August 15, 2024. https://www.
indeed.com/career-advice/career-development/decision-making-skills.

Home Science Tools. "Engineering Kits." Accessed December 8, 2024. https://www.
homesciencetools.com/physics-engineering/engineering-kits-for-kids/?srsltid=
AfmBOorD_vLzjwerzQ7ufno6f73GY-DKWSxeKz4He9u0BXttD41CErGR.

Housman Institute. "Reflective Practice in Early Childhood Education." July 5,
2023. https://www.housmaninstitute.com/blog/reflective-practice.

Hreha, Jason. "What Is a Growth Mindset and How to Develop It in 9 Steps."
Persona. August 16, 2023. https://www.personatalent.com/development/how-
to-cultivate-a-growth-mindset/.

Hulet, Jeff. "Curiosity Exploration: An Evolutionary Approach to Lifelong
Learning." Updated December 6, 2022. https://www.thecuriosityvine.com/
post/curiosity-exploration.

Ibekwe, Osita."20 Conflict Resolution Activities for Kids: Building Harmony
Through Play." OsitaIbekwe.com. August 26, 2024. https://ositaibekwe.com/
conflict-resolution-activities-for-kids/.

IMDB. "Captain America: The Winter Soldier." Accessed December 13, 2024.
https://www.imdb.com/title/tt1843866/.

Indeed, "What Are Analytical Skills? Definition, Examples and Tips." Updated
August 15, 2024. https://www.indeed.com/career-advice/resumes-cover-
letters/analytical-skills.

Jan Peterson Child Development Center. "Exploring Imaginative Play: Nurturing
Creativity in Children." August 17, 2024. https://janpetersoncdc.com/blog/
exploring-imaginative-play-nurturing-creativity-in-children

Jones, Stephanie. "Teaching Your Child About Personal Branding." Personal
Branding Blog. May 9, 2022. https://personalbrandingblog.com/child-
personal-branding/.

Joy in the Meantime. "Family Meeting and Donuts: How We've Improved Our

Family's Communication and Routine." Accessed December 25, 2024. https://joyinthemeantime.com/family-meeting-and-donuts-how-weve-improved-our-familys-communication-and-routine/.

Juraschka, Ryan. "Educational Software for Elementary Students: 9 Expert Picks." Prodigy. July 23, 2019. https://www.prodigygame.com/main-en/blog/educational-software-for-elementary-students/.

Kamaldeep. "Importance of Setting Career Goals (and How to Do It)." Learning Routes. September 19, 2023. https://www.learningroutes.in/blog/importance-of-setting-career-goals-and-how-to-do-it.

Kennedy, Laney. "45 Fun and Clever Brain Teasers for Kids with Answers!" Prodigy. September 30, 2024. https://www.prodigygame.com/main-en/blog/brain-teasers-for-kids/.

Kidsville Pediatrics. "10 Amazing Benefits of Journaling for Kids." December 19, 2024. https://www.kidsvillepeds.com/blog/1257641-10-amazing-benefits-of-journaling-for-kids/.

The Kid's Point. "Encouraging Creative Problem-Solving: Fun Challenges for Kids." September 4, 2024. https://thekidspoint.com/encouraging-creative-problem-solving/#google_vignette.

The Kid's Point. "Mind Mapping for Kids: A Creative Tool for Learning." September 6, 2024. https://thekidspoint.com/mind-mapping-for-kids/.

Kidsville Pediatrics. "10 Amazing Benefits of Journaling for Kids." December 19, 2024. https://www.kidsvillepeds.com/blog/1257641-10-amazing-benefits-of-journaling-for-kids

Klein, Cynthia. "Create a Safe Place for Your Kids to Share Feelings." Bridges 2 Understanding." September 9, 2022. https://bridges2understanding.com/create-a-safe-space-for-your-kids-to-share-feelings/.

Kong Academy. "Goal Setting for Kids & New Year's Resolutions." December 12, 2024. https://www.kongacademy.org/goal-setting-for-kids-new-years-resolutions/.

Koralek, Derry. "Ten Things Children Can Learn from Block Play." National Association for the Education of Young Children (NAEYC). March 2025. Vol. 70. No. 1. https://www.naeyc.org/resources/pubs/yc/mar2015/ten-things-children-learn-block-play.

Kumon. "How to Help Your Kids with Time Management Skills." Accessed December 12, 2024. https://www.kumon.com/resources/how-to-help-your-kids-with-time-management-skills/.

LakeCreek Montessori. "Six Steps to Problem Solving." March 4, 2024. https://www.lakecreekmontessori.org/six-steps-to-problem-solving.

Lake, Rebecca. "Allowances and Kids: How to Build Wealth Habits Early." Investopedia. April 15, 2024. https://www.investopedia.com/guide-allowances-

and-kids-5217591.

Lancia, Gabriella PhD. "Yoga in Education: 7 Poses and Activities for Your Classroom." Positive Psychology. June 28, 2022. https://positivepsychology.com/yoga-in-education/.

Lang, Michael. "Simple Mediation Methods Can Help Children Resolve Disputes." Mediate.com. December 7, 2009. https://mediate.com/simple-mediation-methods-can-help-children-resolve-disputes/.

Latimore, Ed. "7 Ways to Improve Numeracy Skills." Stoic Street-Smarts. Accessed December 10, 2024. https://edlatimore.com/numeracy-skills/.

Learning at the Primary Pond. "How to Teach Students to Compare and Contrast." November 13, 2022. https://learningattheprimarypond.com/blog/how-to-teach-students-to-compare-and-contrast/.

The Learning Center. "Movement and Learning." University of North Carolina at Chapel Hill. Accessed December 29, 2024. https://learningcenter.unc.edu/tips-and-tools/movement-and-learning

Learning Here & There. "How a Timer Can Help Your Kids." Accessed December 12, 2024. https://www.learningherenthere.com/teaching-tips/how-a-timer-can-help-your-kids.

Lee, Brian. "75 Interesting Debate Topics for Kids of All Ages & Grade." SplashLearn. November 21, 2024. https://www.splashlearn.com/blog/interesting-debate-topics-for-kids-of-all-ages/.

Lemonade Day! "9 Engaging Problem Solving Activities for Kids to Build Critical Skills." Accessed February 9, 2025. https://lemonadeday.org/blog/problem-solving-activities-for-kids

Leonard, Daniel. "11 Real World Math Activities That Engage Students." Edutopia. March 15, 2024. https://www.edutopia.org/article/making-math-tangible/

The Life and Times of Ben Weinberg. "Anatomy of a Scene—The Training." Medium. August 15, 2022. https://benjweinberg.medium.com/anatomy-of-a-scene-the-training-bab3cebe95f1.

Listmann, Emily. "How to Create a Study Schedule." WikiHow. February 22, 2024. https://www.wikihow.com/Create-a-Study-Schedule.

Mack, Joshua. "How to Throw a Successful Family Tech Day Event." LinkedIn. March 29, 2016. https://www.linkedin.com/pulse/how-throw-successful-family-tech-day-event-joshua-mack/.

MacPherson, Rachel. "How to Use a Fitness Journal for Goal Tracking." Verywell Fit. Updated March 28, 2024. https://www.verywellfit.com/how-to-use-a-fitness-journal-for-goal-tracking-8424777.

MakerKids. "Robotics for Kids: A Complete Guide for Parents." Accessed December 8, 2024. https://makerkids.com/robotics-for-kids/.

Martines, Alanna. "Wonder Woman 2017." OpenOregon. Accessed December 15,

2024. https://openoregon.pressbooks.pub/dpdfilm/chapter/wonder-woman-2017/.

Martinsson, Gabrielle. "Why Setting Career Goals Is Important for You." Interviewer.AI. February 21, 2023. https://interviewer.ai/why-setting-career-goals-is-important-for-you/.

Marvel. "Peter Parker." Fandom. Accessed December 26, 2024. https://marvel.fandom.com/wiki/Peter_Parker.

Math Geek Mama. "Using Simple Home Projects to Teach Kids Math: Real World Math." September 19, 2022. https://mathgeekmama.com/use-home-projects-to-teach-kids-math/.

Math Unity LLC. "Hosting a Family Math Night Resources." Accessed December 10, 2024. https://www.familymathnight.com/resources/familymathnight.php.

Mayo Clinic. "Exercise and Stress: Get Moving to Manage Stress." Accessed December 30, 2024. https://www.mayoclinic.org/healthy-lifestyle/stress-management/in-depth/exercise-and-stress/art-20044469#

McAnelly, Nell. "How Math Journals Help Students Process Their Learning." Edutopia. December 9, 2021. https://www.edutopia.org/article/how-math-journals-help-students-process-their-learning/.

McGivney, Eileen, and Rebecca Winthrop. "Skills for a Changing World: Advancing Quality Learning for Vibrant Societies." Brookings. May 19, 2016. https://www.brookings.edu/articles/skills-for-a-changing-world/.

McRae, Lauren. "How to Start a New Routine and Stick to It." NorthShore, Endeavor Health. September 25, 2019. https://www.northshore.org/healthy-you/how-to-start-a-new-routine-and-stick-to-it/.

Mediators Beyond Borders International. "Circle Process." Accessed December 13, 2024. https://mediatorsbeyondborders.org/what-we-do/conflict-literacy-framework/circle-process/.

Meier, J.D. "Habits, Routines, and Rituals." Getting Results. Accessed on February 11, 2025. https://gettingresults.com/habits-routines-and-rituals/.

Meredeth, Naomi. "57 STEM Activities for Kids of All Ages and Interests." We Are Teachers. December 11, 2014. https://www.weareteachers.com/stem-activities/.

Microstartups. "Networking for Teens: The Ultimate Guide in 6+ Steps." Updated May 19.2023. https://microstartups.org/networking-for-teens/.

Mikula, Joanne. "Wonder Woman: Female Strength and the Power of Love." The Bi-College News. December 2, 2017. https://bicollegenews.com/2017/12/02/wonder-woman-female-strength-and-the-power-of-love/.

Miller, Gia. "Helping Kids Make Decisions." Child Mind Institute. Reviewed October 30, 2023. https://childmind.org/article/helping-kids-make-decisions/.

Mindomo. "Mind Maps for Kids: Develop Children's Memory and Creativity." October 23, 2020. https://www.mindomo.com/blog/mind-maps-for-kids/.

Minted. "Celebrate in Style: 31 Creative Ideas for Unforgettable Kid's Birthday Parties." January 23, 2025. https://www.minted.com/lp/kids-birthday-party-ideas.

Miss Decarbo. "Compare and Contrast Activity Fun!" Accessed February 9, 2025. https://www.missdecarbo.com/compare-and-contrast-activity-fun/.

Mission Grit. "Teamwork for Kids: Learning the Value in School, Sports and Beyond." Accessed December 12, 2024. https://missiongrit.com/post/learning-teamwork-for-kids.

Modern Recovery. "Conflict Resolution: Definition, Benefits, and Techniques." July 26, 2023. https://modernrecoveryservices.com/wellness/coping/skills/social/conflict-resolution/.

Modi, Priyanka. "Understanding the Importance of a Growth Mindset in Young Minds." Educationnext. December 10, 2023. https://www.educationnext.in/posts/understanding-the-importance-of-a-growth-mindset-in-young-minds.

Moffatt, James. "Encouraging Greater Collaboration: Top 10 Inspirational Stories of Teamwork Success." November 18, 2023. https://www.usebubbles.com/blog/top-10-inspirational-stories-of-teamwork-success?utm_medium=organic&utm_source=www.google.com&utm_content=blog%252Ftop-10-inspirational-stories-of-teamwork-success.

Montgomery Child Care Association. "Exploring Different Art Mediums: Painting, Sculpting, and Crafting for Kids." October 10, 2023. https://mccaedu.org/blog/exploring-different-art-mediums-painting-sculpting-and-crafting-for-kids/.

Morin, Amanda. "8 Social Situations to Role-Play with Your Middle Schooler." Understood. Accessed December 15, 2024. https://www.understood.org/en/articles/social-situations-to-role-play-with-your-middle-schooler.

Morin, Amy. "How to Teach Children Gratitude: It's More Than Just Saying Thank You." Verywell Mind. February 1, 2024. https://www.verywellmind.com/how-to-teach-children-gratitude-4782154

Morris, Connie. "How to Introduce Journaling to Young Children." Edutopia. February 27, 2024. https://www.edutopia.org/article/introducing-journaling-young-children/.

Mostarle. "How Puzzles Help Improve Children's Problem-Solving Skills." August 5, 2024. https://www.mostarle.com/blogs/news/how-puzzles-help-improve-children-s-problem-solving-skills?srsltid=AfmBOopmW6Hg3uzAcabB3W4jI1f p3d3WqadHBC367FdJBlEdEfdk0pnY.

MYDOH. "10 Printable Chore Charts for Kids with Chore Checklist." Accessed December 26, 2024. https://www.mydoh.ca/tools/chore-charts-for-kids-and-teens/.

Naik, Anita. "Examples of Goals for Children (In the Short & Long Term)." GoHenry. Acorns Early. May 24, 2023. https://www.gohenry.com/us/blog/financial-education/examples-of-goals-for-children-in-the-short-long-term.

National Library of New Zealand. "Reading for Pleasure: A Door to Success." Accessed December 8, 2024. https://natlib.govt.nz/schools/reading-engagement/understanding-reading-engagement/reading-for-pleasure-a-door-to-success.

National Sleep Foundation. "How to Make a Sleep-Friendly Bedroom." November 10, 2020. https://www.thensf.org/how-to-make-a-sleep-friendly-bedroom/.

Nebraska Library Commission. "Online Communication & Etiquette." Accessed December 9, 2024. https://nlc.nebraska.gov/Tech/literacy/communication.aspx.

Nemours Kids Health. "How to Talk to Your Child About the News." Reviewed September 2022. https://kidshealth.org/en/parents/news.html

The Nest School. "Healthy Food Rainbow Challenge." Accessed December 30, 2024. https://thenestschool.com/blog/healthy-food-rainbow-challenge/.

Newsom, Rob. "Relaxation Exercises to Help Fall Asleep." Sleep Foundation. Updated February 27, 2024. https://www.sleepfoundation.org/sleep-hygiene/relaxation-exercises-to-help-fall-asleep.

Newsom, Rob, and Anis Rehman. "The Connection Between Diet, Exercise, and Sleep." Sleep Foundation. Updated April 1, 2024. https://www.sleepfoundation.org/physical-health/diet-exercise-sleep.

Nobler, Ronald M. "15 Problem Solving Activities for Students." ClickView. April 23, 2024. https://www.clickvieweducation.com/blog/teaching-ideas/problem-solving-activities.

Northern Illinois University Center for Innovative Teaching and Learning. "Role Playing." Accessed December 11, 2024. https://www.niu.edu/citl/resources/guides/instructional-guide/role-playing.shtml.

Nyabeze, Charles. "The Value of Networking as a Teen: 10 Ways to Make Meaningful Connections with the Right People." Future North. November 24, 2021. https://futurenorth.ca/the-value-of-networking-as-a-teen-10-ways-to-make-meaningful-connections-with-the-right-people/.

Orcena, Alyson, Melissa Vallas, Shikha Verma, Ellen Bloch, Lianne Tendler, and Megan Johnston. "Parent's Guide to Helping Teens Through Sibling Relational Problems." Evolve. January 25, 2024. https://evolvetreatment.com/parent-guides/sibling-relational-problems/.

Our Family Code. "Tallest Tower STEM Challenge with Only Two Materials." July 22, 2021. https://ourfamilycode.com/tallest-tower-steam-challenge/.

Pacheco, Danielle. "Bedtime Routines for Children." Sleep Foundation. Updated

November 8, 2023. https://www.sleepfoundation.org/children-and-sleep/bedtime-routine.

Pandey, Nikhil. "What Is Leadership? Definition, Meaning & Importance." Emeritus India. June 27. 2022. https://emeritus.org/in/learn/what-is-leadership/.

Payton, Gina. "The Importance and Benefits of Comparison Shopping." ShipNetwork. February 16, 2018. https://www.shipnetwork.com/post/the-importance-of-comparison-shopping.

Peanut Butter Fish Lessons. "14 Types of Math Story Problems." Accessed December 10, 2024. https://peanutbutterfishlessons.com/types-of-math-story-problems/.

Pencils to Pigtails. "Easy Science Projects for Preschool and Kindergarten Teachers." Accessed December 13, 2024. https://pencilstopigtails.com/easy-science-projects-for-kindergarten-and-preschool-teachers/.

Perry, Elizabeth. "Get to Know Yourself Through the Act of Self-Reflection," BetterUp. December 21, 2022. https://www.betterup.com/blog/self-reflection.

Phillips-Jones, Linda. "Skills for Successful Mentoring: Competencies of Outstanding Mentors and Mentees." 2013. https://my.lerner.udel.edu/wp-content/uploads/Skills_for_Sucessful_Mentoring.pdf.

The Pennsylvania Leadership Charter School. "How to Create an Effective Study Schedule for Your Children." Accessed December 8, 2024. https://palcs.org/how-to-create-an-effective-study-schedule-for-your-children/.

Perry, Elizabeth. "What Will Make or Break Your Next Role? Find Out Why Teamwork Matters," BetterUp. April 7, 2022. https://www.betterup.com/blog/what-is-teamwork.

Plaxton, Mike. "Reflection: Leadership Lessons Learned as a Child." LinkedIn. June 2, 2023. https://www.linkedin.com/pulse/reflection-leadership-lessons-learned-child-mike-plaxton/.

Prakash, Vaishali. "Responsible Citizenship: An Essential Element for a Better Society." SarvaYog. June 13, 2023. https://www.sarvayog.com/responsible-citizenship-an-essential-element-for-a-better-society/.

Prep Dish. "Easy, Healthy Recipes for Kids to Make (Breakfasts, Snacks & Lunches!). August 3, 2022. https://prepdish.com/meal-planning/healthy-recipes-for-kids-to-make/.

Prep Dish. "Simple Kids Cooking Activities for Different Stages." June 13, 2023. https://prepdish.com/meal-planning/kids-cooking-activities/.

Project Management for Kids. "15 Ideas for Family Team Building." Accessed December 12, 2024. https://www.projectmanagementforparents.com/blog/15-ideas-for-family-team-building.

Quick, Emma. "Happy Place Visualization for Kids." Calm Ahoy Kids. October 17,

2022. https://calmahoykids.co.uk/2022/10/17/happy-place-visualisation-for-kids/#google_vignette.

Raising Children Network (Australia). "Digital Citizenship: Teens Being Responsible Online." Updated February 6, 2023. https://raisingchildren.net.au/babies/play-learning/media-technology/screen-time.

Raising Children Network (Australia). "Nonverbal Communication: Body Language and Tone of Voice." Updated June 17, 2024. https://raisingchildren.net.au/toddlers/connecting-communicating/communicating/nonverbal-communication.

Readability. "Inspire Young Minds: A Comprehensive Guide to Creating Vision Boards for Kids." December 12, 2023. https://www.readabilitytutor.com/vision-boards-kids

ReadTheTale. "Introducing Emotional Intelligence: Teaching Kids to Recognize and Express Their Feelings." Accessed December 12, 2024. https://www.readthetale.com/parenting-tips/learning-development/introducing-emotional-intelligence.

RedClay, Mary, and James Frieden. "Discussion Questions for Use with Any Film That Is a Work of Fiction." TeachWithMovies. Accessed December 18, 2024. https://teachwithmovies.org/discussion-questions-for-use-with-any-film-that-is-a-work-of-fiction/.

The Right Questions. "The 10 Top Life Skills and How to Develop Them." Accessed February 18, 2025. https://therightquestions.co/the-top-10-life-skills-and-how-to-develop-them/.

Ringler, Meghan. "Modern Parenting Challenges: Key Issues Facing Today's Families." Accessed February 18, 2025. https://balancedawakening.com/blog/modern-parenting-challenges-key-issues-facing-todays-families.

Ritchie, Deanna. "How to Teach Time Management Skills to Kids and Teens." Calendar. September 22, 2023. https://www.calendar.com/blog/how-to-teach-time-management-skills-to-kids-and-teens/.

Rocky Mountain Sleeping Baby. "The Role of Nutrition in Your Child's Sleep: Foods That Help or Hinder Rest." Accessed December 28, 2024. https://rockymountainsleepingbaby.com/the-role-of-nutrition-in-your-childs-sleep-foods-that-help-or-hinder-rest

Run Wild My Child. "Starting an Outdoor Herb Garden with Your Kids." June 10, 2022. https://runwildmychild.com/herb-garden-with-kids/.

Russell, Alex. "How Cyborg Became the Heart of Zach Snyder's Justice League." CBR. November 29, 2022. https://www.cbr.com/zack-snyders-justice-league-cyborg-heart-dcu/.

Sala, Rose Gordon. "67 Easy Science Experiments for Kids to Do at Home." Mommy Poppins. August 31, 2023. https://mommypoppins.com/kids/50-easy-science-experiments-for-kids-fun-educational-activities-using-household-stuff/.

Schulze, Sarah. "Habit Tracking for Kids: Does It Work?" Joon. Updated April 6, 2023. https://www.joonapp.io/post/habit-tracking-for-kids.

Schwab, Nick. "29 Interesting Debate Topics for Kids of All Ages." ClickView. February 8, 2024. https://www.clickvieweducation.com/blog/teaching-ideas/debate-topics-for-kids.

Science Is Elementary. "Incorporating Problem-Solving into Daily Routines." Accessed December 18, 2024. https://www.scienceiselementary.org/blog/incorporating-problem-solving-into-daily-routines.

Shea, Alissa Alteri. "Teaching Young Students How to Reflect on Their Learning." Edutopia. July 13, 2021. https://www.edutopia.org/article/teaching-young-students-how-reflect-their-learning/.

SkillPrepare. "5 Ways You Can Use Educational Games to Help Your Child Learn." July 12, 2023. https://skillprepare.com/5-ways-to-use-educational-games-to-help-your-child-learn/.

Smart, James. "40 Problem-Solving Techniques and Processes." SessionLab. June 25, 2024. https://www.sessionlab.com/blog/problem-solving-techniques/.

Spivey, Becky L., M.Ed. "Using Calendar Activities to Extend Classroom Learning." HandyHandouts. Accessed December 10, 2024. https://www.handyhandouts.com/viewHandout.aspx?hh_number=361&nfp_ti tle=Using+Calendar+Activities+to+Extend+Classroom+Learning

Staake, Jill. "11 Helpful Note-Taking Strategies Your Students Should Know." We Are Teachers. December 20, 2023. https://www.weareteachers.com/note-taking-strategies/.

Stallings, Kendall. "Promoting Literacy and SEL Through Letter Writing." Edutopia. September 7, 2023. https://www.edutopia.org/article/letter-writing-elementary-school-promotes-literacy-sel.

Stibich, Mark PhD. "10 Benefits of Sleep." Verywell Health. Updated May 18, 2023. https://www.verywellhealth.com/top-health-benefits-of-a-good-nights-sleep-2223766

Stock, Elizabeth. "Want Your Child to Remember What They Learn? Have Them Teach It." National PTA. June 9, 2021. https://ptaourchildren.org/help-your-child-learn-by-teaching-you/.

Strom, Tanna. "Reading Together." January 11, 2014. Creating Branches. https://creatingbranches.com/2014/01/11/reading-together-a-couple-or-parent-child-activity-to-connect-intellectually-and-emotionally.

Strong4Life. "Learning from Mistakes: Consequences for Kids." Children's Healthcare of Atlanta. Accessed December 26, 2024. https://www.strong4life.

com/en/parenting/setting-limits/learning-from-their-mistakes-consequences-for-kids.

Studentreasures Publishing. "17 Fun Research Projects for Elementary Students." February 26, 2021. https://studentreasures.com/blog/classroom-activities/17-fun-research-projects-for-elementary-students/.

Suni, Eric. "Sleep Diary." Sleep Foundation. June 20, 2023. https://www.sleepfoun dation.org/sleep-diary.

Talbert, Molly. "How to Prioritize Tasks in 4 Steps (And Get Work Done)" Asana. April 4, 2024. https://asana.com/resources/how-prioritize-tasks-work.

Tan, Rum. "Breaking Stereotypes: 5 Creative Digital Projects You Can Do with Your Kids." SmileTutor. September 6, 2023. https://smiletutor.sg/breaking-stereotypes-5-creative-digital-projects-you-can-do-with-your-kids/.

TeachKloud. "Ethics in Early Years Education." December 17, 2023. https://teachk loud.com/early-childhood-education/ethics-in-early-years-education/.

TeachersPayTeachers (TPT). "Grocery Store Math." Accessed December 10, 2024. https://www.teacherspayteachers.com/browse/free?search=grocery%20store%20math.

TeachersPayTeachers (TPT). "Supermarket Scavenger Hunt." Accessed December 30, 2024. https://www.teacherspayteachers.com/browse?search=supermarket%20scavenger%20hunt.

Terry, Bonnie. "4 Steps to Goal Setting for Kids." Scholar Within. December 12, 2013. https://scholarwithin.com/successful-goal-setting-for-kids?srsltid=AfmBOorrt_K71WAnf5ES-a_Rb43ejDpHL9XOP2s2gw Wvz34MWQBZs9jF.

There's Just One Mommy. "Using Pretend Play to Teach Money Skills." January 20, 2017. https://theresjustonemommy.com/teaching-money-skills-math-activity/.

ThinkOrBlue.com. "An Easy Trick to Help Your Child Choose Their Own Clothes." Accessed December 16, 2024. https://thinkorblue.com/help-your-child-choose-their-own-clothes/.

Thompson, Whitney. "Week Five—Spider-Man Learning 'With Great Power Comes Great Responsibility,'" Anchor Counseling Centers. November 15, 2022. https://www.anchorcounselingcenters.com/superhero-blog/week-5-spider-man-learning-with-great-power-comes-great-responsibility.

Tirrell-Corbin, Kristy, PhD. "How to Teach Children about Cultural Awareness and Diversity." PBS Kids/For Parents. August 3, 2015. https://www.pbs.org/parents/thrive/how-to-teach-children-about-cultural-awareness-and-diversity.

Toward Wellbeing. "Emotion Naming Games for Children." Accessed December 12, 2024. https://www.towardwellbeing.com/emotion-naming-games-for-children.

Trammell, Donna E. "Family Meetings—An Important Strategy for Creating Good

Stewards." Bessemer Trust. Accessed December 26, 2024. https://www.besse mertrust.com/insights/a-closer-look-family-meetings-an-important-strategy-for-creating-good-stewards.

twainausten. "Why (& How) to Get Your Homeschool Kids to Journal." Capturing the Charmed Life. June 5, 2024. https://capturingthecharmedlife.com/why-how-to-get-your-homeschool-kids-to-journal/.

Twinkl. "Mystery Activities for Kids." Accessed December 18, 2024. https://www.twinkl.com/blog/mystery-activities-for-kids.

Tynker. "Coding for Kids and Teens Made Easy." Accessed December 8, 2024. https://www.tynker.com/.

University of San Diego Professional and Continuing Education. "A Teacher's Guide to Digital Literary & Digital Literacy Skills in the Classroom." Accessed December 11, 2024. https://pce.sandiego.edu/digital-literacy/.

University of Washington Information School. "What Is Information Management." UW iSchool. Accessed December 11, 2024. https://ischool.uw.edu/programs/msim/what-is-information-management

Vallejo, Michael. "20 Best Cooperative Games for Kids to Foster Teamwork and Collaboration." December 27, 2023. https://mentalhealthcenterkids.com/blogs/articles/cooperative-games-for-kids.

Vallejo, Michael. "25 Best Empathy Activities for Kids." Mental Health Center Kids. April 10, 2023. https://mentalhealthcenterkids.com/blogs/articles/empathy-activities-for-kids.

Vandekerckhove, Marie and Yu-lin Wang. "Emotion, Emotion Regulation, and Sleep: An Intimate Relationship," National Library of Medicine. December 1, 2017. https://pmc.ncbi.nlm.nih.gov/articles/PMC7181893/.

Visions Service Adventures. "21 of the Best Volunteer Ideas for Groups." February 5, 2024. https://visionsserviceadventures.com/blog/best-volunteer-ideas-for-groups/.

Waco Moms. "A Step-By-Step Guide to Vision Boards for Kids." December 31, 2022. https://thewacomoms.com/how-to-create-a-kids-vision-board-with-goal-setting/.

Walker, Stacy E. "Journal Writing as a Teaching Technique to Promote Reflection." National Library of Medicine. Accessed December 16, 2024. https://pmc.ncbi.nlm.nih.gov/articles/PMC1472640/.

Wallace, Bill. "10 Leadership Secrets from Captain America." Selling Power. November 11, 2014. https://www.sellingpower.com/blog/10-leadership-secrets-from-captain-america.

Waters, Erin. "How to Teach the Difference Between Wants and Needs: 11 Ideas to Shake Things Up." Erin Waters Education. Accessed December 14, 2024.

https://elementaryedu.com/2022/07/the-difference-between-wants-and-needs.html.

We Are Teachers. "33 Fun Time-Telling Games and Activities." March 7, 2024. https://www.weareteachers.com/5-hands-on-ways-to-teach-telling-time/.

WebMD. "Benefits of a Teenager Getting a Job." April 10, 2023. https://www.webmd.com/parenting/benefits-of-a-teenager-getting-a-job.

WebMD. "Benefits of Extracurricular Activities for Kids." Reviewed April 10, 2023. https://www.webmd.com/parenting/benefits-extracurricular-activities-kids.

Websults. "How to Teach Website Design to Kids." February 28, 2023. https://websults.com/website-design-kids/.

WebWise. "Digital Literacy Skills: Finding Information." Accessed December 8, 2024. https://www.webwise.ie/teachers/advice-teachers/digital-literacy-skills-finding-information/.

West, Mary. "Math Anxiety." Medical News Today. September 29, 2022. https://www.medicalnewstoday.com/articles/math-anxiety-definition-symptoms-causes-and-tips.

Whalen, Matthew. "6 Volunteer Projects to Grow and Show Leadership Skills." National Society of High School Scholars (NSHSS). January 7, 2024. https://www.nshss.org/resources/blog/blog-posts/six-volunteer-projects-to-grow-and-show-leadership-skills/.

Whole Child Counseling. "Activities for Teaching Kids Good Sportsmanship, Teamwork, and Cooperation Skills." April 16, 2022. https://www.wholechildcounseling.com/post/how-to-teach-kids-good-sportsmanship-teamwork-and-cooperation-skills?srsltid=AfmBOooybFBTznFUjqXqvO8iBgtEM3QJTmjtsBYYdABcDM5DcUn1Umc7.

Wikipedia. "Avengers: Endgame."

Wikipedia. "Cooking Weights and Measures." Accessed December 10, 2024. https://en.wikipedia.org/wiki/Cooking_weights_and_measures

Wikipedia, "Iron Man." Accessed December 19, 2024. https://en.wikipedia.org/wiki/Iron_Man.

Wikipedia. "List of Abstract Strategy Games." Accessed December 19, 2024. https://en.wikipedia.org/wiki/List_of_abstract_strategy_games.

Willis, Judy. "Guiding Students to Harness Mistakes for Learning." Edutopia. May 24, 2024. https://www.edutopia.org/article/power-learning-mistakes/.

Wooll, Maggie. "What is Creative Thinking and How Can I Improve?" BetterUp. June 14, 2024. https://www.betterup.com/blog/creative-thinking.

Wooll, Maggie. "13 Tips to Develop a Growth Mindset." BetterUp. July 26, 2021. https://www.betterup.com/blog/growth-mindset.

Worley, Jamie. "Building Projects for Kids." Real Life at Home. June 25, 2014. https://www.reallifeathome.com/building-projects-for-kids/.

Wyatt, A.C. "Wonder Woman 2017 Movie Review. " Medium. July 28. 2017. https://medium.com/@novelramblings/wonder-woman-review-diana-complexity-strength-b3ba6ab5f2cb.

Your Therapy Source. "Active Listening Games." February 17, 2023. https://www.yourtherapysource.com/blog1/2023/02/17/active-listening-games-2/.

Zaffarano, Kari. "Body Scan Meditation Techniques for Kids." Metro Parent. October 22, 2020. https://www.metroparent.com/parenting/health/body-scan-meditation-techniques-for-kids/.

Zamudio, Noelle. "Involving Children in Family Decisions: Nurturing Shared Decision-Making." Ascension Counseling. August 24, 2024. https://ascension counseling.com/involving-children-in-family-decisions-nurturing-shared-deci sion-making.

EXPLORE OTHER WORKS BY MIKE KLAASSEN

NONFICTION

How to Write a Novel That Matters: Crafting Stories with the Power to Captivate, Enlighten, and Inspire

Third-Person Possessed: How to Write Page-Turning Fiction for 21st Century Readers

Scenes and Sequels: How to Write Page-Turning Fiction

Fiction-Writing Modes: Eleven Essential Tools for Bringing Your Story to Life

HISTORICAL FICTION

Backlash: A War of 1812 Novel

YOUNG-ADULT NOVELS:

Cracks

The Brute

KLAASSEN'S CLASSIC FOLKTALES

Jack and the Beanstalk: The Old English Story Told as a Novella

Cinderella: The Brothers Grimm Story Told as a Novella

The Frog Prince: The Brothers Grimm Story Told as a Novella

Hansel and Gretel: The Brothers Grimm Story Told as a Novella

SUPERPOWER LIFE SKILLS

Superpower Life Skills for Teens with Ambition: How to Master Resilience, Conflict Resolution, Teamwork, Money Management, Critical Thinking, and More to Become Your Best Self

ABOUT THE AUTHOR

Mike Klaassen writes thought-provoking and action-filled narratives about young protagonists confronting significant challenges. His works, including *The Brute, Cracks,* and *Backlash: A War of 1812 Novel,* display dynamic storytelling and compelling character development.

Driven by a passion for continuous learning and research, Mike delved into the art of storytelling, producing a series of insightful books about the craft of writing fiction. These books offer practical guidance for aspiring writers and illuminate the processes behind compelling storytelling.

Fusing his love for folklore with his skill in fiction, Mike initiated "Klaassen's Classic Folktales," a collection that retells ancient stories as novellas. Through this series, he breathes new life into time-honored tales, offering readers of all ages a fresh perspective on these enduring stories.

As a proud father and grandfather, Mike believes each generation encounters unique opportunities and challenges, which inspired him to write *Superpower Life Skills for Teens with Ambition* and *How to Raise Good Humans.*

www.ingramcontent.com/pod-product-compliance
Lightning Source LLC
Chambersburg PA
CBHW060153130626
46556CB00006B/2618